AN UNSPOKEN WAR

AN UNSPOKEN WAR

Eugene O. Charley

ISBN: Hardcover 978-1-4257-7122-5
Softcover 978-1-4257-7103-4

Nonfiction-Based on a true story . . .

What if you grew up in a city/town where racism and prejudice was the native tongue?
What if you felt your life/survival depended on you getting away?
What if you chose the US ARMY as your salvation, yet found that the same issues existed?
Would the life you ran from eventually consume you?
Would you be able to decipher friend from foe?
Could you grow to trust/love one you were taught to hate?
Would you give into stereotypes or evolve to become a better person, one where intelligence outweighs the environment you are subjected to?

Happy Reading, these experiences changed my life. My hope is that they can impact yours in a positive way. Thank You!

Comments are welcomed at unspokenwar@yahoo.com.

This book was printed in the United States of America.

To order additional copies of this book, contact:
Xlibris Corporation
1-888-795-4274
www.Xlibris.com
Orders@Xlibris.com

40643

CONTENTS

CHAPTER ONE

A New Beginning

They all arrived to face their worst fear head-on with a positive attitude: Malcolm, quiet with a no-nonsense demeanor; Jeff, loud and a little disgusted with the mixture of races and togetherness of it all; and Sharon, innocent but in disbelief of the small-mindedness of people when she thought it was just her family. They were all quickly introduced to the fact that no one cares where you are from. The only thing that matters is where you are now: the United States Army. They also don't care what you think because the army is the only way from now on. The new recruits were all herded to a cattle truck and piled on head to toe and, in some cases, on top of each other. As the truck came to a stop at Fort Leonardwood, you could hear a pin drop. They were all speechless, nervous, and afraid of what awaited them outside the doors. Then the doors slammed opened with enough force to pull it off the hinges followed by a loud voice, shouting in a very violent tone, "Get off my bus, you ragbags. Right now, and you better not be the last one off." They began rushing off at a fast pace, so fast that some of the recruits were trampled in the process. After exiting the bus, they were greeted by about ten very large loud men dressed in military fatigues and brown round hats. They were drill sergeants, and they took absolutely no mess from anyone.

"Get in line, you maggots! Get away from me! Over here, over there," was being yelled by each drill sergeant

By now, the young troops were tired from all the rigorous, physically intense drills and wondering what the hell they have gotten themselves into, as they stood covered in sweat. Each recruit was ordered to drop their bags and pick them up, drop them, pick them up over again, which left them exhausted. Then the drill sergeant ordered, "Dump your bags out!"

After the bags were emptied, they took inventory of each item. They called an item, and the recruits would hold it up. The entire process took about forty-five minutes followed by more yelling and running around like chickens with their heads cut off. By now, it was time for chow, and they had worked up a very big appetite. So they marched to the chow hall. Upon arrival, the recruits were given a crash course in education in how to behave in an army mess hall. They walked them through the door expecting a moment of peace but couldn't be further from the truth. As they entered, another group of drill sergeants was waiting inside to welcome them.

"Get up against the wall and keep your eyes on the head of the soldier in front of you," one of the drill sergeant bellowed out. More and more yelling like "shut up" and "don't eye ball me." Random recruits were picked out and made examples of, within this group was Malcolm.

The drill sergeant walked up to him and asked, "What's your name, Private?" and Malcolm sounded off with his name. "Don't eyeball me, son!" yelled the drill directly in his face. Malcolm began to posture in a negative manner by dropping his eyes, slouching his shoulders, and looking away as if to say, whatever. This action brought more attention to him, and other drill sergeants were called over to spotlight him and further antagonized Malcolm.

One drill sergeant asked him, "Do you have attitude problem, Private?"

As Malcolm attempted to respond, he was then asked, "Who are you looking at, Private?"

Malcolm is doing all he can to not say anything and gave off a little smirk, which angered the drill sergeant further. They snatched the food tray from Malcolm's hand and ordered him outside.

"Since you think everything is funny, you can't be too hungry. Get down on the ground and beat your face!" Malcolm looked puzzled, unaware of this terminology. They yelled again, "Get on the ground and start pushing, Private!" Malcolm started doing push-ups. Malcolm, nearing muscle failure, heard a voice through all the yelling. This voice was calm and low in tone yet very stern but not aggressive. "Malcolm," said the drill, "are you going to be a troublemaker?"

"No, sir," replied Malcolm, tired and nearly collapses from all of the push-ups.

"Do you want to give me a hard time?"

"No, sir."

"Then get on your feet, Private, and don't call me sir, I work for a living. Just so you know, I will be keeping a close eye on you. Where are you from, Private?"

"Detroit."

"Detroit!" The drill sergeant yelled out. "Oh, so you're a tough one, huh?"

Malcolm didn't respond.

"Answer me, Private!"

As he attempted to answer, he told him, "Shut up and get in formation with the other soldiers who had finished eating!" As the soldiers started to file out of the chow hall, they were organized and then marched to their new barrack housing.

CHAPTER TWO

New Home

The recruits entered the barracks and were introduced to their new home for the next six weeks. They were divided into four platoons and were led into the building. Each platoon had four drill sergeants assigned. They were all taken to a room known as the rec room, each platoon had their own. While in this room, the head drill sergeant gave them a brief synopsis of what they would expect over the next six weeks. He started by explaining the physical requirements.

"Push-ups, sit-ups, and a two-mile run are essential for graduation. Training will be intense and broken down in the form of classes daily over the course of the next six weeks. It is imperative that you follow the orders given to you and remain alert during training. Rest assured that all of you would not graduate. Better yet, some of you will not make the fourth week. My pledge to you is that I will not send anyone home that doesn't want to go. I believe everyone is equal in the eyes of God and so is everyone in this platoon. This means if you were some 'D' kid looking to get a free ride, I will send you on first thing smoking back to wherever in the hell you came from. If you're some delicate female that thinks someone should carry your bags or some guy who thinks he can be a slacker all of their life, this is definitely *not* the place for you, and I will weed you out. This is a place where boys will become men and girls will become women. Each of you will be responsible for one another, so get used to it." Observing the soldiers' posture, some seemingly falling asleep with their head nodding down, he ordered, "On your feet, soldiers!"

The soldiers were moving far too slowly for his taste, and he ordered them back to the floor and to their feet again, over and over, until they moved at the speed he expected of them. The recruits were then ordered to look at the recruit on his/her immediate left.

"Get to know this person as if he or she was your family member. For instance, if they have a brother or sister, know their name, age, where they were born, blood type, etc., you get the point. You will be quizzed on it. Understand this is not a joke, and these people standing to your left and right may have to save your life someday. So take this as a joke, and I'll take you as one. Now get out of my rec room, you ragbags, and go to your assigned sleeping quarters."

They all jumped up with the speed of light and hurried to their bunks. Briefly after entering their room, the drill sergeant came in and informed them that the way their bed looks before they got in it is the way they should look when they leave—blanket corners folded and tucked tight enough to bounce a quarter off it. Then they were told lights out in ten minutes.

The recruits rushed to get their bags put away and headed to bed, but before most could finish, they heard a loud voice yell, "Lights out!" followed by complete darkness.

The next day proved to be the worst so far as they were awakened at an extremely early hour of 0415. As the recruits sleep silently in their bunks, the drill sergeant violently barged into their rooms turning the lights on, yelling and shouting, "Get the hell out of my bunks, privates, now move it!"

As they scrambled to get their shoes, some being so dazed, actually fell from their bunks to the hard floor. It was at that exact moment that Malcolm wondered what he had gotten himself into along with other soldiers. They were then hurried downstairs outside in the freezing cold of Fort Leonardwood, Missouri, for their first day of training. The recruits now stand outside in the freezing cold, awaiting instructions from their drill sergeants. Malcolm couldn't help but notice a young woman shivering beside him. She was very attractive and, from appearance, had a privileged upbringing. She turned to him and said, "Hello, my name is Sharon."

He replied, "Hi, I'm Malcolm. Nice warm weather we are having, huh." They both began to grin.

At that instance, the drills called them to the position of attention then marched them to the physical training or PT area. Once there, they performed a series of drills including push-ups, sit-ups, and running. At one point, it began to snow, and the recruits just knew they would be marched back inside, but instead they were led on a one-and-a-half-mile run, which ended at the barracks.

Once they returned, recruits were ordered to fall out and hit the showers. They were to return in forty-five minutes dressed in BDUs for breakfast chow. In a flash, they hurried to their rooms and grabbed some personal items before heading to the shower. The bathroom was a mess, with lots of pushing and shoving for a bit of water. A couple of minor scuffles took place but ended quickly. After taking a shower and getting into uniform, they made it to formation tired and restless. The recruits were marched to chow and allowed to eat. After eating, they were led to a series of classes being taught about the ways of the army and survival skills that would aid them in combat. This process would continue on for weeks; with every passing week, they would be allowed more freedoms.

After the first week, they were allowed to call home. Sharon called home.

"Hello, Mom, how are you?"

"I am fine, but your stepfather's health is failing. He's been admitted to the hospital and is on bed rest."

"Will he be okay?"

"I am not sure, but I think you should come home."

"Mom, I want to finish training here first. Dad would understand."

Malcolm called his mom. "Hey, Mom, how is everything?"

"Good. How are you, son?"

"I'm making it. I called to make sure you received the money I sent."

"Yes, I did, thank you. I managed to catch up on some bills with it. You keep your head up in there. So you know, I am very proud of you."

"Okay. Love you, Mom. Gotta go."

On the way back to the barracks, he noticed Sharon looked troubled, and he asked, "Is everything okay?"

Sharon looked at him and asked, "Why did you join the army?"

Malcolm paused a little, put off by the question, but decided to answer, "For me it was not a difficult choice at all. The short answer is either join the army or end up dead or in jail. You see, where I come from, it is hard to earn an honest living and even harder to avoid bad karma. Many of my friends and people I grew up with fell prey to the streets. I refused to go that route. Why did you join? It would appear you don't need to be here."

"If you mean money, you're right. I'm not in need of that. There are other reasons a person would leave home."

"Why?"

She hesitated telling him but really wanted to vent. Noticing the hesitation on her face, he said, "Hey, if you want me to back off, just say it. It's not like we know each other or something. We only spent the past week in hell together, right?"

"You know the funny thing is it seems like I've known you for a while. I don't feel uncomfortable talking to you." Thinking she wouldn't see him again after graduation, she said, "I joined the army because I am from a mixed background, and my mom doesn't want me to learn anything about my heritage. You see my mom uses her money and influence to try and control me, but this way, I have my own and can choose my own path in life."

Malcolm grinned and asked, "What are you mixed with?"

She replied, "Black, silly."

He smiled too and said, "I don't see it."

"My father was of very fair skin, but he was black, his mother and father were also." The two nearing the barracks prepared to part ways.

Malcolm said, "It was nice talking to you, and I hope you find all that you seek on your journey."

Sharon returned the sentiment, saying, "I'm sure you would have made it in here or out there." The two smiled and parted ways.

The next two weeks proved to be a challenge not only physically, but mentally as well. The soldiers are required to be up at 0415 hours for PT. They returned to the barracks at about 0530 hours where they were given thirty minutes to shower and dress in BDU uniform and attend a 0600 hours formation where they were marched to chow. Immediately after chow, they were assembled and marched to a classroom where they were taught about safety, first aid, and combat training all in which they were tested on daily. Malcolm would emerge as an admired person among his peer group, finishing first in almost every event. He mostly keeps to himself and doesn't want any added attention brought his way. When Sharon got the news that she would have to leave, she walked up to Malcolm on break between classes. He could see she was bothered.

"Are you okay?"

"No, my stepfather died last night. I wouldn't leave training to see him when he was sick."

Malcolm could see how hurt Sharon was as her eyes were filled with tears. He attempted to comfort her by saying, "Listen, you did what you felt you had to do. You did not know the outcome would be this. I know it is hard, but the worst thing you can do is blame yourself. Just go home and be strong for your mom, she'll need you the most."

"I know. It is just hard, you know?"

"Yeah, I can imagine, but I am sure he is proud of you for following your dreams."

"I doubt it. He thought what I was doing was stupid."

"You know I've found that people don't always say what they think but instead what they believe will change your mind about a thing."

"You know you are probably right because he left home at an early age too. Wow! Thanks, Malcolm, this is exactly what I needed to hear. You are deep and a good friend."

"Oh, you see me as a friend?"

"Yes, I do."

"Then that is what we are." She hugged him briefly and walked off.

The last week was upon them, and rumors of the best of the best were out. Soldiers from different platoons that were the best in their graduating class would be recognized before their units. As Malcolm was being recognized, he kept hearing another name associated with his. This soldier's name was Jeff. He was also a top performer and led his platoon in many events. There was another name that came up often but referred to in a more negative light, the name was Travis, and it would appear he loves attention. Jeff and Malcolm never met but were regarded for finishing at the top five of their class. They all went on to graduate and headed to the next training station of AIT at Fort Lee, Virginia.

CHAPTER THREE

Personalities Clash

Travis, Jeff, and Malcolm all arrived at the same time at Lima Company, the in-processing company for new arrivals. The new recruits were headed, with their bags, to their temporary quarters.

There was a light-skinned young black male carrying his bags up, and Travis referred to him as a samba. The young recruit kept walking, not really knowing what the word meant. But it did catch the attention of Malcolm who was following not too far behind. He knew exactly what it meant and gave Travis a look that would melt steel, as if to say watch your mouth. Malcolm knew at that moment Travis was going to be trouble, the kind he didn't need. All the soldiers proceeded to become acquainted with their new homes.

A few days later at 2100 hours, which was lights out, as some recruits slept peacefully in their bunks, most lay awake thinking about memories of home. Travis, on the other hand, had a hard time finding rest in his sleep; he was hunted by past relationships. This experience aided in Travis's current mind state. The time has now come to 0430 hours, and it's PT time. There will be a test conducted on push-ups, sit-ups, and a two-mile run. During the first half of the events, the drill sergeant teamed up Malcolm and Jeff, one would count while the other pushed up and held each other's feet during sit-ups. Jeff initially walked over to Travis, who was teamed up with another white solider, and asked the other guy to switch. As he finished asking, the drill sergeant walked up to him and asked, "What the hell do you think you're doing, Private!" He stood puzzled. "Did you hear me, Private?" "Yes, Sergeant!" Jeff returned back to where Malcolm was standing with a half grin on his face. The drill ordered them to get in the push-up position, Malcolm doing so while still grinning. Jeff asked him in a bellicose tone what he found so funny. Malcolm looked into his eyes, and before words could exchange, the drill yelled, GO! And they began doing push-ups. The group finished and made quick work on the sit-up event. They now moved to the two-mile run. As Travis and Jeff moved into start position, Malcolm has taken a spot in front of them. "You see that" asked Travis. "Yeah," replied Jeff.

"Now I'm sure he's one of those boys from the field."

Malcolm turned toward him with a look of rage and anger, but before he could react, the race was off. They were now in a race for time. As the race got under way, Jeff and Malcolm immediately pulled ahead of the pack and finished within the top five of the group while Travis almost failed to even qualify. After the last recruit crossed the finish line, the drill sergeants ordered everyone to hit the showers. No sooner than the order was given, Malcolm rushed in to await Travis's arrival, who was still sluggish. He walked into the locker room laughing, joking, and had completely forgotten about the comment he made before the race had begun. As his foot crossed the entrance, a very angry recruit, with a calm and no-nonsense demeanor, greeted him. Travis tried to play tough by saying, "Move out of my way," but before the words could completely exit his mouth, Malcolm grabbed him very tightly around the neck and pulled him to the floor on the side of some lockers. Seeing the overwhelming fear in his eyes, Malcolm, in a low yet forceful tone, told him, "If you ever speak of or about me in a disrespectful way again"—he growled—"let's just say it will be the last time." He then threw Travis to the ground and walked away.

Jeff arrived just as Malcolm walked off and was in disbelief at the fact that Travis did nothing to defend himself. Not knowing the whole story, he asked, "What happened?"

"Nothing. Darkie just got a little upset at his true history."

"Why didn't you hit him?"

"I slipped, but don't worry . . ."—his eyes began to change with a far away look—"before this is all over, I'm going to kill that nigger, you can believe that."

Jeff felt a chill go down his spine as he watched Travis utter those words and remembered a similar look on the face of his father many times. It scared him in a way because he knew Travis meant those words, and that's not what he joined the army for. He could have stayed home for that. After they showered, they were assigned to their permanent quarters for the next eight weeks.

The rooms were issued out by last names. Malcolm's last name was Coleman, and Jeff's last name was Colton; therefore, they became roommates. This was a blow to Jeff and Travis, who were hoping to become roommates. Jeff even approached the drill and asked, "Can I have another roommate, preferably Travis?"

The drill asked, "Why?"

"I don't really get along with Malcolm."

The drill again asked, "Why?"

In an effort to buddy up with the drill, "Would you want to room with one of *them*?"

The drills face turned red, and anger immediately followed. He ordered Private Colton outside. "Private, to your knees! Start pushing up . . . down . . . up . . . down . . . On your back, start sit-ups. Up . . . down . . . up . . . down." The drill smoked him for two hours straight, and while doing so, he let him know that it was his kind he would be insulted to room with, and that the US Army had no place for that type of attitude.

Jeff returned to the barracks huffing and puffing up the stairs to his new room where Malcolm had picked the bed by the window and was just nice and cozy in his room. Jeff was upset that Malcolm had already settled in and very upset of the fact that he had to sleep in a room with a guy who tried to rough up his buddy. He thought he should put him in his place.

"What makes you think the bed by the window is yours?"

Malcolm stopped reading his soldier's book and said, "Because I'm lying on it." He began to joke and said, "Possession is three-fourths of the law." Smiling and turning back to his book.

This angered Jeff further, so he decided to raise the stakes by asking, "What ghetto did you come from?" He didn't answer. Malcolm recognized the game that's being played. As he saw Travis perched in the doorway, he then turned and faced Jeff but still no response. He continued ignoring Jeff.

"What are you a coward?"

At this point, Malcolm closed his book and challenged him by asking, "What do you want to do? All I hear is your mouth running. You seem real soft to me, little lady."

Jeff became enraged and got very loud, yelling, "YOU DON'T KNOW WHO YOU ARE FUCKING WITH, YOU BLACK BASTARD!"

The other soldiers, hearing the commotion, rushed in to investigate the noise.

Malcolm was still calm sitting on his bed until Jeff called him a black bastard and invited him to step outside the room. This comment upset other black soldiers as well. With a slight grin on his face, he stood and followed behind Jeff. When Jeff got just beyond the exit, Malcolm slapped him in the back of the head and told him, "Have fun!" as he slammed the door and went back to reading. Leaving him outside with the angry soldiers who knew why he was being smoked earlier that day.

Once in the hall, one soldier asked Jeff, "What's your beef with the skin tone?"

"Mind your business."

The solider again asked, "What's up?"

"Get the fuck out of here." As those words left his mouth, other soldiers walked up, and a brawl started in the hall. But before any real damage was done, the drills heard the loud commotion and ordered the entire platoon outside for a smoking session.

The drill walked up to Malcolm, "What happened?"

"Nothing I am aware of." This further angered the drill.

Private Johnson who confronted Jeff in the hall earlier asked Malcolm, "Why didn't you kick Jeff's white ass?" No reply from Malcolm. "So are you scared to fight or something?"

"How bad do you want to know?"

"Oh, so you'll fight one of your own with no problem, but you'll let these white boys run all over you."

"Look, man, if you want to start some united black front because of a couple stupid white boys, fine, that's your thing just leave me out of it. If I thought whipping his ass would have helped, I would have, but it wouldn't, so what's the use? Now we're all down here sweating like pigs for nothing. Plus I bet he learned more by me not whipping his ass, because deep down that's what they expect us to do. So please keep your comments to yourself and leave me the hell alone, because believe me ain't nobody messing this army thing up for me, be he black or white, I got too many people depending on me."

After the smoking session was over, they were dripping wet from sweat. They were ordered back to their quarters and confined to their rooms until lights out. Jeff was ordered to go to the TMC and get checked out for minor injuries. When he arrived, he was ordered to sign in and take a seat, which he did. After about thirty minutes, a sergeant called his name directing him to room 2. As he walked in, his face lit up like a Christmas tree, for he was looking at the most beautiful woman he had ever seen. She was a gorgeous recruit in training to be a nurse. She was about five feet and five inches, pretty blond hair, deep blue eyes, and full lips. An almost island appeal with light bronze skin as if the perfect tan.

"Hi. I am Private Sharon. What is the problem today?" She started checking his vital signs.

Still in shock by her beauty, he stumbled over his words. "I . . . I fell . . . while doing PT."

She laughed and said, "Oh, that was you out there with that platoon being smoked, you guys looked so cute," as she blushed trying to get Jeff to relax.

Just before he could work up the nerve to say anything of a personal nature, the doctor walked in and ordered Private Sharon to another room for vitals. He then attended to Jeff and sent him back to his barracks. By the time he returned, it was lights out, and Malcolm was lying calmly in his bed as if asleep. Jeff just fell into his bed consumed with thoughts of Sharon, which kept him smiling all night long.

The next morning, the platoon was ordered to attend a consideration of others class after breakfast. During breakfast, Jeff told Travis all about Sharon and how he couldn't wait to see her again. Travis was overwhelmed with thoughts of the class and how everyone would act. They arrived at the class with the rest of the soldiers. Jeff was pleasantly surprised to see Private Sharon. Travis, with an angry look, was awaiting a chance to speak, and Malcolm, calm yet curious to see what this class would amount to, took it a joke in his opinion.

CHAPTER FOUR

The Racial Debate

Sergeant White was an attractive white female instructed to give the class on consideration of others. This was a subject she was very passionate about, and it came across as she would speak. She looked out in the crowd and saw everyone sitting with his or her race classification—she immediately wanted to break them up into diverse groups. She told them all to get up and mix it up a bit, but even after she spoke, most of them picked the same seating arrangements. Malcolm picked a seat off to himself since he viewed himself as a loner. This diverse group included many different races: blacks, whites, Latinos, Asians, and mixed combinations. When Malcolm went to sit, Pvt. Sharon Sinclair, who remembered him from basic training, noticed Malcolm and moved to sit by him. This left a confused look on the face of Travis and angered Jeff.

The class began with Sergeant White giving an overview of what racism is and the negative effects of it, and that "we have no place for it in the army."

"This is an oral class, and participation is not an option. To the best of your ability, I want you to feel free in expressing whatever you want, and address it in an educated manner. Remember we are soldiers. Show patience and respect for other soldiers' comments and responses. Does anyone have something to say?"

Travis was all too anxious to get his two cents in. He started by saying, "As far as coloreds, I like the Old South where they knew their place and for the Spanish people, we are in America now, so speak English because I get tired of hearing all of that gaba gaba when I walk by them."

"What!" yelled out a black and a Hispanic soldier.

Standing, the Hispanic soldier said, "Say it in my face, puto!"

The black soldier yelled out, "That is a coward's comment just like he is."

Sergeant White then calmed the crowd, "At ease! Travis, this is not an arena for blunt stupidity. If you have something of merit to say, then say it; otherwise shut up." She changed the scope a little by asking an Asian solider in the class, "Private Kim, what are some of the stereotypes you've faced?"

"Well, one of the common statements made is we all know karate, or we are so passive and don't want to ruffle any feathers."

"Private Jeff, what do you think about what he said?"

"I agree, we do think that, but some of them do act that way."

"The key," said Sergeant White, "is that some is not all, and we can't assume anything these days."

As she finished her statement, Private Travis said, "Don't forget chinky eyes . . ."

"Drop and start pushing!" Sergeant White ordered.

Private Johnson blurted out, "There's always a good old piece of country trailer trash in the area."

Which inspired Jeff to say, "And I thought your momma couldn't make it." This surprising statement got a laugh from most of the class, black and white alike.

Sergeant White told Travis to return to his seat. After this, the class had broken the ice, and the discussion continued on with participation from everyone except Malcolm.

Private Sharon insisted that "if people weren't so judgmental of others and concentrated on making themselves a better person, then we could truly come together." Sergeant White agreed, and for the most part, everyone applauded Sharon's statement. At this point, Sergeant White noticed that Malcolm was not involved with any of the class and asked, "Private Malcolm, do you have anything to add?" which brought him unwanted attention.

He replied, "No, not really."

"Why not?"

"Because this class doesn't really interest me."

"Why do you feel this way?" And before he could answer, Jeff blurted out, "I guess you don't have no problems with white people, huh? Ha-ha!"

Private Johnson jumped in with a cheap shot of his own, saying, "He does but he believes that if he ignores it long enough, it won't affect him, right?"

This caused some commotion and Sergeant White yelled, "At ease!"

Malcolm then stood up and said, "It seems to me if we really wanted to come together, we are asking the wrong questions. Instead of drawing out and exploiting the differences, as we seem to be doing with questions like, what are some stereotypes? Or how do you feel about being this race or the other? we should instead ask what can we do to become a people, meaning one because we do share the fact that we are human."

Sergeant White felt like Malcolm was somewhat challenging her method, so she asked, expecting a no response, "Do you think you can do a better job with the class?"

"Sure," he replied to her surprise. "All we need to do is not focus so much on what makes us different, but what commonalities we share and there are many."

A Hispanic soldier asked, "What do you mean?"

Malcolm explained, "We all need to eat to live, right? And although we all eat at different times and different foods, we are not judged by that, and it's something we share in common. We all need water, shelter, basic clothing, and acceptance from friends and family. So why can't we focus on some of these issues, which may lead us to the conclusion that we are not so different after all? In short, why can't we focus more on the fact that we have skin, instead of always talking about the color or texture of it? Basically, as was more than likely said by the original people on this earth, 'I am man, you are woman, and we are human.' Period."

The class just stared at him in complete shock with a look of surprise upon their faces. Some recruits feeling a sense of pride or renewed faith in the fact that all are created equal. Malcolm just walked back to his seat not feeling any different from when the class started, because to him this class made no difference to the way the soldiers viewed each other.

Sergeant White said, "Remember it takes only one to make a difference. Anyone of us can make a difference." and continued on with the class.

As the class let out, Sharon walked up to Malcolm and said, "I didn't know you were so passionate about this topic."

He replied, "I'm not. But the truth is the truth." And he walked off, letting her know it was good seeing her again, and that they would catch up later.

Jeff then approached her and asked, "Do you remember me?"

"Of course," she said with a large smile across her face.

"How do you know that guy?"

"What guy?" She asked.

"The one giving the I-have-a-dream speech." He laughed.

"You talking about Malcolm? We went to basic training together. That statement you just made was almost offensive. I thought what he said was right on target with what's real. It was interesting seeing you again. Have a nice day." Sharon walked off. Jeff dropped his head and uttered "Damn" to himself.

The soldiers all walked to the chow hall for their dinner meal. Malcolm sat back, enjoyed the meal, and watched his surroundings. Jeff came in, talking to Travis about his conversation with Sharon and how she got upset with his comment. Travis said without a thought, "She's probably a nigger lover, you know so-called free spirit."

Jeff looked at Travis in a kind of disbelief that he would use words so harsh, especially about a woman he liked. He then started to wonder just how angry this guy was about the world. Just before he could say something to him about it, they were at Malcolm's table, and Travis started putting on a show. He started clapping loudly and, with great sarcasm, told Malcolm, "That was a great speech! No, really it moved me."

Malcolm said nothing. He briefly looked up and continued eating, but he did notice that Jeff was not very conformable being a part of what Travis was doing. A drill sergeant noticed the commotion and told the two to take a seat and eat before they are no longer afforded the opportunity. They quickly complied.

After eating, they headed back to the barracks. Travis walked with Private Watson while Jeff elected to walk alone so he can reflect on all that happened that day. More importantly, he was wondering how he could face Sharon again. He entered the room not really knowing what to expect being in a room all night with Malcolm, a black guy whom he had already pissed off. As he entered the room to his surprise, Malcolm was sitting calm reading a book. This further confused him because he was taught that all blacks were stupid and didn't want to learn even if you tried to teach them. Instead, they were gangbangers and drug dealers with no regard for human life. Yet here sits this young black guy, sitting and reading and not being made to.

Jeff looked at Malcolm with an alarming look across his face and asked, "Why did you slam the door on me like that?"

Malcolm looked him in the eye and said, "Look, whatever problems you have are within you. You need to work them out because they can't be with me, you don't even know me. So I'm not going to bail you out of dealing with your own self-issues by kicking your little ass."

Jeff quickly replied, "You must be mistaken because the only ass that would have gotten kicked was yours."

Malcolm laughed, "You know the funny thing is you believe that. Look, truth is I have no beef with you or that punk-ass Travis you run with. For me, the army is a way out of troubles you couldn't begin to imagine. And I'll be damned if I let a couple of wannabe skinheads fuck this up for me. Got it?"

"Yeah," Jeff replied. "You'll be surprised at what I understood." After that statement, the drills yell lights out and not another word pass between the two that night. That night they both lie awake, thinking of the other's position.

What seemed like minutes after falling to sleep, the soldiers awoke to the loud sounds of drills yelling, "Get up and get in my formation now!" As they made it to formation, they were made aware that they will be taking a physical fitness test that day for record—which is a test of push-ups, sit-ups, and a two-mile run.

Drill Sergeant Ashford jokingly said to the soldiers, "This test should be no problem since you had all that energy yesterday, so let's get started." Immediately after beginning, it seemed Malcolm and Jeff got the attention of the drills with their great athletic ability. They quickly stood out. Jeff was finishing his push-ups at 104, sit-ups at 110, and two miles at nine and half minutes while Malcolm finished his push-ups at 135, sit-ups at 100, and two-mile run at ten minutes flat. Sharon also finished in the top percentage of the female soldiers. Travis failed to qualify on the sit-ups or the run, which attracted some negative attention. He didn't want embarrassing utters of him being weak from fellow soldiers. After a grueling PT test, they were given downtime to shower and take care of personal items or needs.

Malcolm elected to use some of his time to call the love of his life, Michelle, who is away in college. The two of them had been together since eighth grade and knew they were soul mates. The phone was answered by a sleepy voice, "Hello."

His reply brought her to her feet. "It's me, baby girl."

Michelle now wide-awake after hearing his voice asked, "How are you, sweetheart? I miss you so much it hurts."

"I'm okay, just tired right now. I miss you too, more every day."

Michelle expressed her concerns for her love and sensed he was a little stressed. Yet knowing the type of man he is, he would not tell her thinking it might be a burden on her studies. "Is everything okay, baby? Do I need to come hurt somebody for my baby?"

Smiling, Malcolm replied, "No, I'm good. I just wanted to let you know I love you, and you were thought of today."

She began to cry and said, "I love you too. You are my heart and soul, okay?"

He assured her, "I am not going to mess this up. I will see this thing through to the end no matter what the outcome."

"I know you will, I know you will." On that note, the conversation ended, and Malcolm hurried to the PX to pick up some supplies.

Jeff also used the phone to call home; he talked to his mother, letting her know he's doing fine. "I am seeing a different world far different from the one I was accustomed to."

His mom replied, "That's great because there is much for you to learn about life, and I'm so proud of you." His mom knew exactly what her son meant and, in a way, wished she could have taken the journey many years ago herself.

Jeff heard his father in the background. "Hey, put Dad on."

His father in a drunken state replied, "I don't have anything to say to you. You are an embarrassment to me." That troubled Jeff but didn't surprise him one bit, and he quickly got off the phone.

He then went to the common area to relax. Travis came in shortly after complaining, "The PT test is unfair, and it caters to the blacks and browns for they are good at that anyway."

Jeff told him, "Shut up and sit down. When are you going to blame yourself because you are running out of other people to blame?" Thinking of his father, Jeff saw Travis was behaving just like his father and how he had been taught. The phone call, hearing his mom's frightful voice, and his dad refusing to even speak to him, reinforced his reason for joining the army. Also, reminding him of the changes he needed to make. Though it wouldn't be easy, he knew he owed it to himself to open his mind to the world around him. Yet more importantly, stop confusing ignorance with bravery. Just as he was finishing his conversation, Sharon walked up and heard the whole conversation and was very impressed. Jeff told Travis, "Look I'll help you pass the PT test, but I've heard enough of that shit from my pops, so just cut it. Okay?"

Travis gave him a look of disbelief and said, "Man, what's eating you?" Jeff just walked out of the room. Sharon admired Jeff for saying those words, and she knew they were from the heart, but she didn't say anything at that time; she just kept walking to her barracks.

CHAPTER FIVE

Combat Training

The soldiers returned from their personal time to find that the next day they would team up on a weeklong field assignment where they would have to depend upon each other for survival. The soldiers all returned to their quarters, each reflecting and thinking of back home. Malcolm could see that Jeff was troubled, so he asked, "Is everything alright?"

Jeff responded with haste, "What do you care?" and quickly turned over and attempted to fall asleep. Malcolm just shook his head and turned to a sleeping position as well.

The next day was quickly upon them, and they both head down toward formation. As they walked, Jeff turned to Malcolm and said, "I didn't mean to be rude last night. I just had something heavy on my mind."

Malcolm looked at him and replied, "Don't worry about it."

They headed to formation without another word passing between them. Staff Sergeant Hanson held the formation. He was a very large white man from Texas with a very intimidating demeanor and had an even worst stare. When this man spoke, everyone moved at a high rate of speed. Staff Sergeant Hanson's task was to ready them for a possible combat environment with a week of simulated training exercises. He informed them, "In combat no one solider can make it on his/her own. This is and always will be a team battle. War could come at any time, and all we can do is train and ready ourselves for the challenge. In combat, you never know who will be the person to have to save your life, so it's best to be respectful of all your fellow soldiers. Just remember the word *team* and you'll be fine."

Staff Sergeant Hanson proceeded to position them into teams. Travis stood next to Jeff in hopes of being paired up with him. His goal was successful as he and Jeff were placed on the same team; Malcolm was teamed up with another group same as Sharon.

Staff Sergeant Hanson gave directions. "Complete an obstacle course as a team, and you must finish together in a timely fashion. The first team back is the winner." Malcolm was appointed the leader of his team as Travis was appointed the leader of his. This was clearly a competition, and the first team back would be the winner.

Malcolm immediately huddled his squad to gather info from everyone to come up with a game plan and a positive speech, which was a display of great leadership that the drills noticed.

Travis on the other hand took this as an opportunity to bark orders and demand respect.

"Jeff is number 2 in charge."

Private Wilson, a black solider, asked, "Can I be the point man?"

Travis just laughed at his request and responded in a loud tone, "Never!"

Saying to Jeff under his breath, "Like I would let one of them lead us."

Staff Sergeant Hanson heard all of this but, at this point, said nothing as Travis smiled at him, in hopes of support for his attitude.

Staff Sergeant Hanson ordered them to the start position. "Remember that although you are a team, it will be a team of two off at a time." The race started, and two teams were neck and neck, but Malcolm's team was very well organized and quickly moved ahead because of their attitude, endurance, and the fact they wanted to win as a team. Shortly after the race started, Travis's team began to fall apart with no real direction, some finishing before others and having no idea where their teammates were. Their downfall was the fact that he wouldn't accept input from the team and instead take them on what he believed to be a shortcut, which got the team lost. There was a third team in their platoon led by Private Hilton, which finished fifteen minutes after the first team led by Malcolm. The drills congratulated the two squads and began waiting for the third squad to come in as they showed up one, two, and three at a time. By this time, the whole squad was in a state of disarray and yelling at one another. Travis and Jeff tried to take charge by telling them to shut up, but Private Wilson told them, "Shut up and I am tired of listening to the both of you."

The rest of the team agreed shouting, "Yeah!"

Travis tried one more time to take charge, "At ease, soldiers!" But it fell on deaf ears—no one paid any attention. Another twenty minutes had passed, and the soldiers started to speculate on what might have happened.

Malcolm said, "With Travis leading them, they are probably back at the start point because he's as backward as they come!" The soldiers started to laugh.

Drill Staff Sergeant Hanson jumped in Malcolm's face. "Shut up, all of you! This is not a laughing matter. You think it's funny that your fellow soldiers are lost in combat or may be hurt? You better start taking this matter a lot more seriously because one day it may be you lost somewhere. Now since you seem to have it all together, lead your squad back on the course and don't come back until you found each and everyone of those fallen soldiers. Oh, and you only have fifteen minutes to do it or your squad will be pulling guard duties until we leave this training exercises. ARE WE CLEAR?"

"Yes, Drill Sergeant!" replied Malcolm with a very angry look on his face. He then looked Malcolm in the eye and said, "We don't leave anyone behind you, understand?" At this point, Malcolm viewed him as another redneck mad that one of his own can't hack it, and it left Malcolm very upset, viewing Drill Staff Sergeant Hanson as having a hard-on for blacks.

Drill Staff Sergeant Hanson, on the other had, was very proud of Malcolm and the way he commanded his squad but felt he needs to understand what all for one really means.

Malcolm led the squad back looking for team 2. They first bumped into Travis and Jeff.

Travis asked, "What are you guys doing here?"

Malcolm replied, "We came to bring your squad in. So where's the rest of your squad?"

"We don't need any help from you."

Malcolm said, "I could care less what you need." Malcolm took his squad and continued on, leaving two soldiers to escort Jeff and Travis—one being Sharon, who walked and talked to Jeff the entire way back.

As they walked, Jeff told Sharon, "You know that day in class, I never meant to offend you. I was just kidding around."

Sharon told him in a stern tone, "Some jokes are not funny at anytime or put in anyway."

"You're right. I apologize."

"Forget about it."

"No, no. Please allow me to make it up to you. Would you go out with me the weekend coming up after training?"

"Sure, why not."

Shortly after, Malcolm found the rest of the squad and headed back. As Travis, Jeff, Sharon, and Private Whitt walked to the finish point, they were quickly approached by an angry Drill Staff Sergeant Hanson, who asked in a loud and violent tone, “Where is the rest of your squad?”

They just stood in fear as he ordered them to drop and start doing push-ups. Travis tried to explain, “I had one of those troublemakers in my squad.”

“What do you mean?” he asked as Malcolm and the rest of the two teams walked up. Staff Sergeant Hanson seemingly ignored Travis and asked Malcolm, “What happened?”

“Nothing,” he replied.

“Drop!” yelled Staff Sergeant Hanson. “How did some of your team come in while others of you were still out there?”

Malcolm attempted to cover for everyone by saying, “Travis and Jeff were so close to the end, I just sent Sharon and Whitt to show them the rest of the way while we found the rest of the team.”

This earned Malcolm a lot of respect among the soldiers, for they knew the truth. The story went over well as they were told to recover (stop doing push-ups). But Travis’s ego wouldn’t allow it, so he blurted out, “He’s lying we refused to go with him.” Jeff looked at him in disbelief.

“What!” bellowed Staff Sergeant Hanson.

“We didn’t need his kind of help? If it weren’t for that Private Wilson, we would have been back a long time ago. He continually undermined my authority within the squad.” Private Wilson attempted to defend himself but was quickly told to at ease by the drill.

By this point, Drill Staff Sergeant Hanson was fed up with Travis and his ways. He walked up to him, got in his face, and yelled at a high tone, “Private, if you wanted to be a skinhead, this is the wrong uniform, and if I hear any more of your bullshit, we are going to go out back and have a private conversation without words. There is no place for hate in the United States Army. Are we clear, Private?”

“Yes, Staff Sergeant,” responded Travis. He then ripped the squad leader’s patch from Travis’s arm and walked to the front of the formation.

“Fall out to chow, with exception of my squad leaders.” Travis stood there puzzled.

“You are relieved of duty. Not only did you fail to complete the course, your ability to lead is below standard. You could learn from Malcolm and Hilton.” This angered Travis greatly. “Jeff, you will stay as acting squad leader.” Drill Sergeant Hanson let them know what his expectations would be over the course of this week. “First platoon will be number 1 in your training, and I will not accept any excuses from anyone. HOOH!”

The soldiers echoed, "HOOH!"

The dismissal angered Malcolm, but what could he say? The truth is the truth. As he sent the squad leaders to chow, he pulled Malcolm to the side for a brief conversation. "I am very impressed with the way you handled the mission, but you need to stop being such a loner." Malcolm just stood silent and listened. "I know you could be a great leader, and I see the soldiers already respect you, but the question that remains is, can you effectively lead them? Go to chow and think about what I said."

By now, news had traveled to the other platoons about first platoon's mishaps in the woods and Travis's attitude about black soldiers. Jeff was labeled guilty by association although he said nothing. As the squad leaders walked into chow, they were surprised to see the soldiers joking and laughing with Private Dave leading the pack, a black soldier from Travis's old squad. He asked Travis, "Do you need help finding a seat or is my color preventing you from listening to me although it's obvious I know more than you." Travis just kept walking, looking down at the floor.

Private Hilton told the soldiers, "At ease." as she walked by. Malcolm said nothing but noticed very down looks on some of the soldiers' faces. Malcolm suggested to Hilton, "Let's all do something as a platoon because it will make this weekend that much easier to deal."

"That's a good idea. What do you have in mind?" she asked.

"How about we all go to the sports bar and just play pool and dance."

"Sounds great!" she replied. "We'll bring it up tomorrow after formation."

After chow, Travis looked for Jeff, but he blew him off to walk and spend time with Sharon, whom he had grown very found of. That night, Travis was haunted with dreams of a girl he loved very dearly before joining the army. She was tall with picture-perfect skin, her eyes deep blue with long blond hair. She was from his hometown, and he hoped they would be together forever. One day, he went up to her college to visit unannounced and saw her in the arms of another guy. Just as he saw them in his dream, the horn sounded, and he woke up breathing heavily in a sweat. The soldiers all hurried down to formation.

CHAPTER SIX

A Night Out

The soldiers were assembled in formation, and the drills gave the safety brief for the weekend. Once released from formation, Private Hilton told everyone to meet at the sports dome after chow. At chow, Sharon and Jeff agreed that this would be the perfect place for their first date. Malcolm delayed his trip to the party to call his love to let her know how much he really missed her. Private Hilton arrived first with a few other soldiers laughing and joking about training so far. Malcolm concluded his conversation with Michelle and headed to the party.

By now, everyone has arrived, mingling and socializing with one another. Travis chose not to go, still upset about being dropped as a squad leader. He refused to be around people that would laugh at him or view him as a loser. Instead, at a neighboring bar, drinking, he plotted a way to get revenge on them.

Malcolm walked in, looked around, noticed everyone was having fun, but they were still sticking to their own races, with the exception of a few. He also saw Sharon and Jeff off to themselves laughing and playing; he smiled and moved deeper into the party grinning and talking to fellow soldiers.

Hilton saw Malcolm. "Hi, Malcolm. Everything is going fine. Everyone is here except Travis."

"That's no surprise," replied Malcolm. They laughed.

Sharon called Malcolm over, "How things are going with you?"

"Fine, but as I said, I don't want to intrude."

"Yeah, he doesn't want to intrude." Thinking he may have an interest in her.

Sharon looked at Jeff. "Don't be silly, besides don't you know each other?"

Jeff replied, "You could say that, we share the same room."

"He's no intrusion," said Sharon. "We're old friends from basic, right?" She noticed the tension between the two and grabbed them both by the arm and led them to the pool table, challenging them to a game.

Jeff jumped at the opportunity. "You may be able to beat him, but you don't stand a chance with me."

"Jeff, you and Sharon have fun. I'm not feeling pool right now. You two look good together."

Jeff smiled as Malcolm walked off, stopped him and said, "Thanks."

"Forget it." Malcolm answered then looked at Sharon, "my money's on you."

Jeff then asked Sharon, "How well do you know him?"

"We were in the same company in basic."

"Oh yeah, how was he there?"

"Pretty much the same way he is now—keeping to himself, pissing off the drills, and earning the respect of soldiers around him."

"Sounds like you know him."

"Well, not the way you are implying. We had a conversation once and found we have some things in common."

"What could you possibly have in common with him?"

Sharon looked him in the eyes. "You really need to learn to look past color because it will blind you from seeing the world. Why don't you try talking to him? I bet he's different from anything you could have thought." Jeff stood with a puzzled look, thinking she might be right. Sharon interrupted his thoughts, "Now quit trying to take my mind off this game, let's play." They both laughed it off and started to play pool.

Malcolm found his way to the dance floor and danced a little. He started to notice that as the night went on, the friskier the female soldiers were beginning to be toward him. He first thought nothing of it, but one grabbed his mini-me, and he knew that was his cue to leave. On his way off the floor, one of them asked, "Hey, Malcolm, can we meet up later?" He politely said, "No, thank you, I love my girl."

He then exited the party and headed to the barracks. On his way, he saw a soldier in a group pointing and laughing, so he went over to see what it was.

What he saw made his eyes open twice the size, his jaw dropped in disbelief, and a slight chuckle exited his lips. You see, Travis had gotten himself drunk and attempted to join the party to ruin the fun. But as fate would have it, he passed out against a nearby building and pissed on himself. This was what everyone found so funny. Malcolm quickly stopped laughing and thought, *He is still a member of my platoon*. "Okay joke's over, keep moving."

He then went back to the party, told Jeff about his boy for help. "We need to get him back undetected by the drills." Jeff agreed.

On the way back, Jeff asked Malcolm, "Why didn't you just leave him here? You don't even like him. Why are you helping him? And don't give me that squad leader junk because I know you don't believe that bull."

"You're right, Jeffrey."

"Don't call me that."

"Okay, Jeff, you're right I don't like him at all. I also don't dislike him either."

"What?"

"He means nothing to me one way or the other."

"He's ignorant, prejudice, and a very weak person. A year or two ago, I would have probably beaten him to within an inch of his life for some of the things he's said."

"Oh yeah, what's changed?"

"Not what. Who? Me. I'm not that person anymore. I've learned to deal with my anger. I won't let what someone else does influence what I do anymore. Meaning if you say something and I react to it, then in essence, you've controlled the situation. I view that as weakness, and I will not succumb to it anymore. You asked me why I'm doing this—because I judged a man wrong." He thought of Staff Sergeant Hansen. "He said some things I didn't want to hear at the time, and I labeled him. Shortly after, I found myself to be wrong. So in essence, I'm doing this for that reason. Okay by you, Jeff?"

"Yeah, okay by me."

"Good. Now be quiet, we have to sneak past the CQ."

They successfully got him to his room and shook hands for a job well done. As they were shaking hands, Travis began to sober up and asked, "Jeff, what the hell are you doing?"

"Saving your ass." And the two walked out.

They parted ways. Malcolm went to his room while Jeff returned to the party in search of Sharon. On the weekend, the soldiers have an option of sleeping in quarters or renting a room. Jeff got a room being optimistic of his date.

By the time he returned to the party, it was over. Looking out over the room, he heard a voice saying, "Over here" as she stood waving at him. Sharon waited for him anyway, which was a pleasant surprise for him. He quickly ran to her side, the two embraced in a passionate hug. "It was very thoughtful of you to help take Travis back to the barracks like that."

"How thoughtful?" he asked with a boyish grin on his face.

"Thoughtful enough," she replied as she kissed him on his left cheek. "Now will you walk me to my barracks? It is kind of late."

"It would be my pleasure, beautiful lady."

They began to walk and talk, getting closer and closer to one another. They arrived at the barracks each expressing joy for their first date. Jeff asked, "Do you see another date in the future for us?"

"Definitely."

They stood speechless for a moment both wanting to kiss but too nervous to do so. They finally embraced in a nice hug, and on the release, they engaged in a long passionate kiss. Jeff stood breathless even after the kiss.

Sharon replied, "Thanks for everything." and went to her room.

Jeff waited until she was out of sight and yelled, "Yah-hoo!" then went to his room, and he saw no need to go off post if he had no company.

Jeff returned to his room glowing and smiling as he saw Malcolm on the bed reading.

Noticing Jeff's behavior, Malcolm figured he wanted to talk, so he put his book down and asked, "What's up?"

Jeff was dying to tell someone and was willing to talk to Malcolm. He started by saying, "She is so beautiful and intelligent . . . you know? Her eyes, her lips—man, everything about her I like."

"Calm down, playboy," said Malcolm. "So it's fair to say you like her then."

"Man, that's an understatement."

"Good luck. I wish you both the best."

"Thanks, but I got a question for you."

"What?"

"Well, I couldn't help noticing some kind of bond between the two of you."

"Oh yeah?"

"What's up with that?"

"Nothing. She and I shared some very personal words between each other and found that we're not so different. In a sense, we both have unique reasons for joining the army."

"What does that suppose to mean?" Jeff said in a loud tone.

"Relax, high speed," said Malcolm. "You know a few days ago, you and I had never passed words, now you have so much to say. So tell me, why did you join up for this?"

Jeff clammed back up and said, "None of your business. You know Sharon thinks you're deep, I think you are just full of shit."

"Hey, you're the one with the need to talk. I didn't ask to hear your whining."

"Whatever," said Jeff.

As Malcolm returned his "Whatever," they both turned away from each other and assumed a sleeping position.

CHAPTER SEVEN

What Do You Stand For?

The next day, Sunday, was fast upon them, and Jeff couldn't wait to see Sharon at the chow hall for brunch. As he headed to eat, he stopped to call his mom and let her know he's okay. After his phone call, he saw Travis moping around the halls.

"Are you going to chow?"

"Why? So I can be the butt of the jokes again?"

"Man, you need to lighten up. Look no one knows what happened."

"Oh what? You don't think Malcolm told everyone?"

"You know what, maybe he did but I doubt it."

"What do you mean you doubt it, are you buddies or something?"

"Naw, far from it. Man, you coming or what? 'Cause I'm out, see ya."

"Okay wait up." They left together.

Malcolm took time to call home and talk to his mom, which was always an emotional conversation. You see, Malcolm had assumed the role of man of the house since he was fourteen years of age, and joining the army changed nothing. He still sends his mother whatever he has to pay bills if needed. He even gave her complete access to his bank account so if she needed something, she could get it right away.

"Everything is okay."

"I'm so proud of you. I love you."

"I love you too!" he said and got off the phone. He then headed to chow.

By now, Jeff and Travis were already there. They spotted Sharon and went over to sit with her. Sharon and Jeff began to smile and converse, laughing and joking about their date. They were continuously interrupted by Travis's annoying need for attention, making negative comments about different races of soldiers as they walked in. His comments were not loud enough for them to hear, but that really pissed off Sharon and surprisingly Jeff too.

Sharon asked him, "What makes you think you are so much better then everyone because believe me you're not."

"I'm just glad I'm white, that's all. Hell, the blacks yell their proud shit all the time so why can't I? I'm just saying I'm proud of my race, aren't you?"

"You know what, Travis, all my life I've been around weak little cowards like you who try to judge other people but can't stand up to a true self-evaluation of themselves. Because if you did, I don't believe you would be happy with whatever it is you are."

Travis was angered by these strong words from a woman who doesn't know him at all and asked, "Who the hell do you think you're talking to?"

Jeff stepped in, "Hey, why don't you both just calm down?"

Sharon looked at him and said, "Is that all you have to say?" Furious Jeff didn't jump to her defense and put Travis in his place, Sharon stood from the table and said to Travis, "You are a racist, idiot! And, Jeff, I don't know what you stand for, but you need to make a decision because you're right on the line and you can't stay there. Choose a side and take your true form. You see, courage comes from knowing something is wrong and having the guts to stand against it. When you understand that, give me a call. Good-bye!"

While she was walking out, Malcolm entered. "Hey, Sharon."

"Hi." Sharon answered and continued to walk past him with a look of anger on her face. He noticed tears forming in her eyes as she passed by.

Jeff just sat speechless, not fully understanding why she got so upset. They all finished chow and awaited recall formation at 1700 hours. The soldiers started to gather for recall formation, Jeff anxiously awaiting a chance to see Sharon to apologize for his lack of sensitivity to the matter. As they were called to attention, he saw her out of the corner of his eye.

The drill sergeant ordered them, "Get your eyes to the front, and pay attention! At ease." He told them how important this week of training was. "This task will determine how well you work as a team in a combat environment. You should take it very seriously because I will be watching all of you. I will announce my squad leaders after they are selected. You will follow their orders to the letter or deal with me, and you don't want that. When I give the order to fall out, everyone will go to your rooms and pack all of your field gear. There will be a check of your gear at 0500 hours, so don't disappoint me. That will be all, soldiers, get a good night sleep because you will need it. FALL OUT!"

After they were released, Jeff rushed over to Sharon and asked to talk to her for a minute, but she not only ignored him, she walked away without even looking in his direction.

Travis saw the way she treated him and walked over. "Man, forget that bitch."

Jeff grabbed him by the collar and pushed him into the wall. "Don't you ever call her that again. Do you understand me?"

"Yeah, man, calm down. I didn't mean anything by it." Jeff let him go and walked off to his room.

Malcolm was already there packing up his gear. Jeff starts packing very frustratingly, slamming things around. Malcolm tried to ignore him after he saw what happened. But Jeff made it impossible by kicking things and even stepping on some of Malcolm's gear.

"What the hell is your problem?"

Jeff became more upset and asked Malcolm, "What, you got a problem or something?"

"Yeah, you stomping around this room like some pissed-off schoolgirl with no prom date." This enraged Jeff to the point he took a swing at Malcolm, missing and catching a nice right from Malcolm, followed by a hard push, knocking him to the floor. Jeff jumped back up and rushed to him, causing Malcolm to hit his head on a cavalier helmet. Malcolm was free by this point, and he pushed Jeff off of him and started swinging, connecting with his jaw and rib cage, asking Jeff, "Is this what you wanted?"

"Yeah," Jeff replied, connecting with a right of his own.

Malcolm in a rage started to choke him very tightly around his neck. Jeff attempted to free himself by punching Malcolm, but he won't stop. "Dumb, redneck."

Jeff started to lose consciousness as Malcolm was thinking of the problems he had on the streets. Malcolm began to release him, and Jeff started to cough and then laughed, saying, "Man, that's a hell of a grip you got there. You should see a counselor about anger management or something."

Malcolm looked at him grinning and said, "You know, you are one crazy white boy. With a questionable right hook." and joined him in a laugh.

CHAPTER EIGHT

Defenses Come Down

They both continued joking while they attempted to tend to their bruises. Malcolm looked at Jeff and asked, "What the hell was all this about anyway?"

"I fucked up with Sharon bad. One night we were kissing, now she won't even look at me, and it's eating me alive."

"Why?"

"Because Travis said some stupid shit and pissed her off."

"How long are you going to put up with that asshole, anyway? Let me ask you something, you walked a very thin line on this race thing, you got a problem with black people or what?"

"Man, it's like this, I grew up in a small town where white power was the native tongue. You were either with it or against it, and you better not be against it. My father used to beat up my mom daily after getting drunk or high. When I turned ten, he started beating on me too. It seems I was never good enough for him." His eyes began to water. "He would tell me things his dad did to blacks and even Latinos when they got lost in their town. The thought of it disgusted me, so I spoke out against it at seventeen years old, and he beat me so bad I was hospitalized for two weeks. Could you imagine your own father doing that to you? So when I got well, I saw a recruiter and signed up right after graduation. He tried to stop me, but I told him that if he ever touched me again, I would kill him, and we haven't spoken since. So although I'm not Travis, we share the same damned upbringing, and if you haven't lived it, you could never understand it."

Malcolm replied, "I feel you. You see my life was no picnic either. My pops chose to bail out when I was only four years old. I grew up in Detroit, and it's no place to raise kids, I tell you that. I was always in trouble for one thing or another. In the '80s, either you were selling drugs or on them. Only a few people had the good factory jobs. I watched my mom work herself to death, trying to put food on the table, so what was I to do. I had to fight daily going to school and coming home. So I started selling and was good at it, got the protection I need for my family and me. You see I love my mom to death, and I could see she couldn't do it alone. I remember for my seventh grade year of school, I had three pair of pants. I've seen so much death, I was sure I'd be dead myself by now. My mom would never accept a dollar from me and even kicked me out of her house. I turned to the streets. It just became too much for me, and I didn't like the person I was becoming. One night sitting in the spot, I got shot twice, and I had nowhere to go but home. My mom took me to the hospital, and on that day, I promised her before God I would turn my life around, and that's why I joined."

"It seems we both have come a long way, but it's cool."

The two give each other a mutual headshake, and for the first time, they have a mutual respect for one another. They finished packing their bags and lay down for the night.

Malcolm told Jeff, "Don't worry about Sharon, it'll work itself out, and my bet is, you and Travis don't have as much in common as you think. And I bet you don't share the same demons either." The lights went out, and they lay thinking until they fell asleep.

The next day, Drill Sergeant Hanson came to their floor personally at 0400 hours and called out, "Inspection!"

Now everyone must bring his or her field gear to formation so that it can be checked and accounted for. Travis noticed Jeff and Malcolm helping each other out, and it disgusted him to watch. He went up to Jeff and said, "What's up?"

"Same old shit." Jeff answered and kept packing.

They continued with the inspection, and as they were packing their items up, Sharon walked nearby their position. Jeff immediately got nervous, Malcolm told him, "Calm down. I'll handle it. How are you doing, Sharon?"

She looked over and greeted, "Hello." She was surprised to see him and Jeff standing together.

"I hope we all end up being in the same squad."

"You can't be serious." Malcolm said, knowing he's including Jeff. "I don't want to be around those two." Sharon answered, referring to Travis and Jeff. "And I would think you felt the same way," she added and walked off.

Malcolm turned to Jeff and said, "Man, you must have really pissed her off, but don't worry we can fix it later. Let's go."

Travis stood nearby listening with a strange and devious look on his face.

Drill Sergeant Hansen announced his squad leaders who were Malcolm, Hilton, and Private Whitt. This was a surprise to most who thought Jeff was a shoo-in for the job. Whitt was a very small white solider, who obviously led a very sheltered life. The order of the squads remained the same with the exception of Private Wilson, who was placed in Malcolm's squad; Travis and Jeff remained in what was now Private Whitt's squad.

Travis saw this as an opportunity and went to work on Private Whitt right away. "We need to stick together because there's not many of us here you know." Whitt not really understanding what Travis meant, replied, "Okay."

On the first day, the platoon had to march to their field site, which was twenty miles away. They arrived tired and barely able to stand. Some couldn't make it and were put into the back of a five-ton truck. They were given only a ten-minute water break and were ordered to set up their tents and secure their perimeter. By now, nightfall was fast approaching, and fatigue had set in on all the soldiers by this point.

The drills noticed them dragging and whining; they immediately got in their faces, yelling, "What the hell are you doing? Get it together, Privates! You can rest when you're dead! The enemy is not resting, why are you! You better get this area secure, or no one will sleep tonight. We'll run drills and pull mass guard duties!"

The soldiers started to hustle a lot faster. They managed to complete their mission a few minutes after nightfall hits. Their sleeping arrangements were two people to a small tent, composed of one shelter half apiece making the tent. Now they were safe within the confinements of the perimeter. They began to work out sleeping arrangements. Females would sleep with females and males with males. Squads forming a large triangle with command in the center separated them. Malcolm shared a tent with Wilson, Travis and Jeff shared, and Sharon was allowed to share with Private Hilton although they weren't in the same squad due to an odd number of female soldiers.

As they lay awake, unable to sleep, Wilson started to speculate about what the training would be the next day; Jeff and Travis didn't have a whole lot to say to one another but good night. Sharon, on the other hand, used the time to vent.

"I like Jeff, but I don't understand why he hangs around a guy like Travis. It's so obvious he's a negative influence. It pisses me off when he goes along with Travis's bullshit. If he doesn't change his ways and soon, then I am going to leave him alone because I can't be with someone who acts that way."

Hilton listened and then offered advice, "It's obvious you have some pretty strong feelings for the guy, or it wouldn't get to you like this. You have to realize that the world is not perfect. I see Jeff is actually trying, but it's not as easy for everyone. I don't think you need to give up on him, instead search your heart and make him search his own as well to find out if it's something worth working for at all."

Sharon somewhat in shock of the great advice she received just said "Thanks," and the two fall asleep.

Jeff couldn't sleep, lying awake, thinking of ways to steal back Sharon's heart but was interrupted by moans and violent cries coming from Travis.

Travis was having nightmares or better yet the same nightmare of something that happened in his past involving his past love, which would keep his heart cold and bitter forever. He finally woke up in a ball of sweat, just shaking and looking around franticly. Jeff just looked at him for a minute then asked, "Are you okay?"

CHAPTER NINE

Planted Deception

Travis took a moment to gather himself and began to tell Jeff his haunting past that he can't escape in his sleep. He started by saying, "I see you and Malcolm talking a lot about Sharon. I warn you to be careful, my friend." Jeff looked puzzled.

"I was in love once to a beautiful little hometown girl named Rosary. Man, she was my high school sweetheart, and I was going to marry her. I was working in the factory trying to help put her through college—you know make sure she had what she needed. After she was there for a semester, she started acting different. She said, 'Maybe we should just be friends because of the distance between us.' So I showed up unannounced one day to her campus. She acted all scared of me, so I said, 'What's up, baby?' She said, 'You shouldn't be here.' I told her I loved her. She replied, 'I don't love you anymore.' I asked 'What?' She answered, 'I met someone else.' Then I asked again, 'Who?' Her reply was 'Don't worry about it.' I then noticed a locket around her neck that had not been there before; I snatched it off. 'What's this?' What I saw in that locket was enough to make any red-blooded American's skin curl.

"What was it?" Jeff asked.

"I saw a picture of her kissing a nigger all hugged up. I just snapped. I slapped her across the face and left. I was so messed up behind that I joined the army to get away from it all, but it still follows me."

Jeff replied, "Man, that's some deep shit. Was it the fact that he was black that really got to you?"

"Come on, man, you may be on this liberal shit now, but could you really imagine one of those motherfuckers sticking your girl?" Travis saw that he had Jeff's attention again and started to lay it on thick. "I tell you watch that Malcolm. They are not to be trusted. Have you ever noticed how they are around each other? You think he's helping you, but he's probably helping himself."

Jeff took a moment to reflect and asked, "You think?"

"Ay, just watch out because they love white women."

Jeff wanted to tell Travis he was wrong, but he couldn't help thinking about it. Thinking that if that was the case, Malcolm had the perfect opportunity with him in the same squad as Sharon. Then he just shrugged it off as bullshit and went to sleep.

The next day would prove more exhausting than the first. They had to undergo an obstacle course, which involved climbing, running, low crawling, and even a gas attack. The squad leaders had to successfully lead their troops through together and in a timely fashion, and no casualties were to be left behind. This was an event the entire platoon would undergo at the same time. The catch was that each squad would start at different points. This means somewhere in the course they would cross paths, but they would all have different ending points. Private Whitt was no leader; he didn't really know were to begin, so Jeff took over the squad, and for his first time as a leader, he is a natural. He began organizing and giving orders, and the squad all seemed to agree with. This actually put them at the front of the other squads from a time standpoint.

Malcolm, on the other hand, was having bad luck because his starting point was a gas attack that hit them completely by surprise. When the CS gas was released, the squad panicked and started to scatter. Malcolm gave the signal for gas, and ordered them to stop and put on their protective gear. He continued to put on his gear, and cleared and sealed his mask, and then slowly started to gather everyone up. Most of them had put their masks on by this point and headed back to the start point. As he gathered up his squad, he noticed that Sharon was nowhere in sight. He ordered the squad to continue to the next rally point, and as they started out, he heard someone choking and gasping for air. He ran to their aid and discovered it's Sharon. He immediately put her mask on and took her to the gas-free area. She was still gasping and was disoriented, so he lay her down and checked her vital signs. He began asking her questions to help bring her around. Everything seemed to be okay, but the commotion got the attention of other squads and the drills as well. So they began to rush over to see who was hurt.

Just as Malcolm was helping her up her hand around his neck and his hand around her lower back, Jeff and Travis walked up. Travis gave Jeff a look, but he was already furious to see the two of them in such a compromising position. He immediately got the wrong idea and ran off. Malcolm saw them from the corner of his eyes but didn't understand why he would run off like that.

Travis caught up to him and said, "I told you, man."

Jeff simply replied, "You were right. I was so stupid."

"You're not stupid. They are just more devious and sneakier than us, you couldn't have seen that coming. Don't worry, I'll make him pay."

Jeff noticed a cold and faraway look in his eyes, remembering only one other face where he'd seen that look—in the eyes of his father. Jeff told him, "Don't worry about it. I fight my own battles." Travis mumbled under his breath, "Who's talking about fighting?" and walked off.

As they both headed back, the drills have brought order to the situation. Sharon was taken to the nurse's tent to be checked out while the rest of the platoon finished the mission. As the day was coming to an end, the platoon was brought together and informed on how they performed throughout the course. They were also given a safety awareness class so that they could avoid further incidents while on this field exercise. They were then ordered back to their tents where they received personal time to write letters and read sent letters. That night was pretty calm. Everyone reflected on what had happened that day, thinking that this was serious not only for his or her graduation, but possible survival as well.

The next day came with little or no sleep. The soldiers were still battered and bruised from the day before, awaking sluggish and restless, which was exactly what the drill sergeants wanted.

Drill Sergeant Hansen yelled out, "Formation!" After they formed up, he led them on a ten-mile road march. This march would lead to a weapons range, where they would be tested for accuracy with an M16 rifle. Seeing as how they were tired hungry and even bruised up, this would be a perfect war-type scenario to see if they could engage the enemy under duress. They all lined up on the firing range one squad at a time. First up, White's squad where Jeff and Travis did very well shooting in the top 10 percent of the qualifying score. The next up was Malcolm's squad, and on the way in, Travis was coming out. He looked over and aimed his finger as if firing a gun at Malcolm, saying, "Bang" and walked off with a half grin on his face. Malcolm looked at him in the eye and brushed shoulders with him as he passed and kept walking. On the range, Malcolm also did well.

Now the range was set up. There were two soldiers; one was firing and the other was watching the target and letting their partner know where the round went. Malcolm and Sharon were partners on the range. Malcolm used this time to try to help patch things up with her and Jeff.

"Jeff is miserable. All he talks about is getting you back."

She smiled and said, "I really like him too, but if he can't get past the race thing, we can never be together."

"I don't really think that will be a problem."

She looked strangely at Malcolm and asked, "Why are you on his side? You're supposed to be on my side." She smiled.

"I don't believe I'm on anyone's side."

"Okay, why the change of heart about him?"

"I don't believe I've changed, I just didn't know him at first."

"And you do now?"

"Well, let's say we've talked, and he's an okay guy."

"Well, if you think he's okay, then maybe I did miss something."

"So you'll give him another chance?"

"Yeah, why not. I'll talk with him when we finish this field assignment. I'll let him sweat a little."

"Good. I know he'll love to hear that."

By now, they're done with the range and were on their way out. As they walked back to formation, Sharon looked at Malcolm and said, "I thought you would be the last person to speak up for him. You are full of pleasant surprises. Thank you." As she said thank you, she reached over and hugged him. Jeff, who was walking up, saw the two of them hugging and flipped out. He ran over and pushed Malcolm away from her. Sharon yelled for Jeff to stop, but he took a swing at Malcolm.

Malcolm moved and grabbed Jeff, asking him, "What the hell is your problem?"

Jeff said, "Why you trying to steal my girl? I thought you were going to help me, not backstab me."

Malcolm started to laugh and asked, "Where did you get a stupid idea like that?" looking in the direction of Travis who was standing nearby. "Slow down, slugger, I'm not trying to steal her. I just sealed the deal for you. She said she would give you another chance that's why she hugged me."

"What?"

Sharon nodded yeah with a slight smile on her face. He immediately apologized to Malcolm while Sharon who was strangely turned on by his act, walked over to Jeff and said, "First of all, I'm not your girl. Second, I can appreciate what you attempted to do here, but the only problem is you have your real friends mixed completely up, and it's sad that you can't see that by now." With that, she kissed him on the cheek and walked off.

He then turned to Malcolm and said, "Man, I can't believe I did that. I just saw the two of you close and listening to Travis I just got jealous. My bad. We still cool?"

Malcolm replied, "It's all good. No harm, no foul. But how long are you gonna let this guy be your excuses?" The two shook hands and headed to formation together.

After taking the long road march back, they turned in for the night. Jeff lay with a smile and a glow about Sharon. Travis asked, "What's with you?

Jeff said, "Sharon wants me back, and you were wrong about Malcolm. He puts it all together for me."

"You really believe that shit, huh."

"Yes, I do," he said with a smile.

"So I guess you have a new friend now?"

"Yeah, you could say that."

"No matter how close you get to the dark man . . ."

"Watch your mouth," said Jeff with a stern voice.

"Okay, okay. Touchy too, huh? Just remember, no one will watch your back like one of your own." The two turned away from each other and went to sleep.

The next day was beautiful. The sun came up as the soldiers had already started their day. The training today would be different from what they'd been doing up to this point. Today, they would work together as a platoon. Drill Sergeant Hanson called a formation at 1200 hours for first platoon and told them exactly what they would be doing for training. He told them,

"Listen and listen good. Today we will be engaging the enemy. The enemy will be second platoon. We will wait until lights out and break through their perimeter security. Need I remind you, this is just a training. You are to follow orders to the letter. On the battlefield, your lives will depend on it. Now, second platoon will know we are coming, but they will not know when and how. It's your job to be unseen and undetected and breach their defense with enough numbers to take the platoon. I warn you. It will not be easy, and if caught, you will become a prisoner of war (POW). I again tell you, this will take teamwork, it is important that we understand that. Now I just have one more thing to say. Squad leader Private Whitt informed me that he wants to step down. I now appoint Private Jeff as the new squad leader. That will be all. I will brief my squad leaders, and they will brief you. Fall out!"

He instructed them on the best ways of possibly attacking second, but also let them know the decision would be theirs. He reminded them, "You are the heads of the whole operation, and teamwork is essential. Any one solider can give your position away so watch them all closely. Good luck, Privates!"

They went back to inform their platoon of their roles in the attack. The soldiers noticed togetherness about them the moment they returned. They also informed them that they would be wearing mile gear, which beeps when you are shot. When they finished briefing them, it was just about sundown. They chose to enter the perimeter from three different points at one time. They wished each other luck and headed to the start point.

CHAPTER TEN

The Attack

As the sun started its final descent, they started their attack. It was the perfect time, for second platoon was caught completely off guard, expecting the attack much later. They had just finished chow. Most of the squad was walking to their guard posts. Malcolm's squad moved in from the front while Jeff's squad came in from the rear position, and Hilton took a side angle to help corner the platoon. At first, it seemed everything was going great; all three squads had effectively got past second platoon's defenses. Malcolm's team took five POWs while Hilton's had taken three of their own. Jeff's squad, on the other hand, ran into trouble; it seemed Private Travis had a problem taking orders and started an argument with Jeff. In doing so, it gave away their position. This argument got the attention of Private Dave from second platoon and some of the other soldiers in that squad. They immediately started to fire on them. Jeff's squad quickly returned fire.

By now, everyone's mile gear was beeping, but no one would stop firing. During the chaos, Travis grabbed a large rock and hit Private Dave in the face with it. Dave ran over to Travis with a right cross connecting with his jaw, and fellow members of his squad joined in. Jeff noticed the entire squad beating on Travis and ran to his aid with the help of a few of his own squad, but they provided little help, for most didn't want to help Travis at all. By now Malcolm has made it to their position and saw what's going on. He immediately shielded Jeff, who was bleeding from the head. He also noticed that as soon as the fight shifted to Jeff, Travis used the opportunity to run off. Malcolm was struck in the head and started swinging. They seemed very reluctant to hit Malcolm, who caught them most by surprise even defending

Jeff. The drills all ran over and dropped CS gas to break up the mob of soldiers. While they were gasping and attempting to put on their masks, Drill Sergeant Hanson gathered up the first platoon and took them back to their field and demanded to know what happened. Jeff was taken to a medical tent where Sharon tended to his bruises.

Drill Sergeant Hanson asked Malcolm, "What the hell happened out there?"

And before he could answer, Travis blurted out, "That damn Private Dave and his squad attacked me and Jeff for no reason!"

Drill Sergeant Hanson looking at him strangely, asked, "Okay. But how did they detect your position when you were already past the guards?" Travis stood speechless. "Well, at best, you all stuck together." Malcolm looked at Travis with disgust and walked off to check on Jeff.

He walked in and attempted to lift his spirits, "Man, you were head butting their fists like I've never seen!"

Jeff was laughing in pain, "Go to hell."

"I see you're in good hands here, so I'll see you later."

"Wait a minute, Malcolm. Man, I owe you big for that."

Malcolm smiled and said, "Forget it."

Jeff replied, "No, I'm serious. You didn't have to help me. Hell, I went to help Travis even he ran off."

"Oh, you saw that?"

"Yeah, I did. I really want to say thanks, man."

"Okay already, you're going to make Sharon jealous. Seriously, I'm sure you would have done the same for me, so just heal up, slugger."

Travis walked in after Malcolm left. Jeff asked, "What the hell do you want?"

Travis with a surprised look, asked, "What?"

"You fed me all that stick tighter than blood shit, then you ran off when I tried to help you. Fuck you, man!"

"Oh, I see you got your new soul brother, so you turn your back on your own kind."

"Look, coward, we ain't blood, and if we were, I'd get a transfusion." Travis walked out enraged by Jeff's words. Sharon could see how upset Jeff had become, so she gave him a kiss on the head and a nice hug.

"You've really changed since we first met, for the better. I mean, you were very judgmental and opinionated of people and things that were either different from you or that you just didn't understand. You seem to be at peace and show more consideration for the world around you."

"You know, it's amazing the difference a little time in the presence of the right people can make. I now believe we were destined to meet and be together. I truly do love you, and thank you for the positive influence and gentle nudges that have helped me grow at this point." She shied away with a childlike grin. As he stood to walk toward her, Drill Sergeant Hansen walked into the tent and ordered them both to formation.

In formation, Sergeant Hansen said, "For the most part, training was a success. We've undergone some key survival and combat training that will aid you on the battlefield. So you guys should be proud of that."

The soldiers replied, "Hoo ya!"

"However, due to the ignorance displayed by a select few of your fellow soldiers, you all will be privileged to a consideration of others class, which is our last day in the field. That'll be all, fall out and get some sleep."

That night was quiet. The soldiers used the time to reflect on everything that happened. Travis turned to Jeff in the tent and apologized, but Jeff just listened in silence saying nothing in return. Travis said, "Man, I didn't mean to leave you. I was trying to find something to pick up—a stick or rock—I wasn't leaving. Do you forgive me?" Jeff still failed to respond, no more words passed between them. Malcolm slept with his own demons of defending this white boy and even striking a young black man like himself, something before joining the army he never would have done.

The morning came of what will be their last day in the field, so they were picking up a lot of their personal items and were heading to formation. The drills gathered them all to formation. They were first congratulated on a good week of training, saying that for the most part, everything went well. The drills went on to say that the incidents that occurred was believed to have a large part to do with racial tension or, in other words, ignorance. "So go to chow and after you return, we will have a class addressing the issues." The platoon fell out and headed to chow.

While there, Jeff and Sharon sat together, locked in intense conversation about the coming weekend. Malcolm sat alone, thinking about his love Michelle and how training is almost over. He and Jeff locked eyes with a mutual nod to say hello. Travis too was sitting alone, wondering how he lost his best friend and feeling betrayed. In his mind, he related this loss to the loss of his sweetheart to a black man. So even though he felt betrayed by Jeff, his anger was mostly focused on Malcolm. As they finished eating, they headed back to formation. They were ordered to form up in an informal formation, which means they were to form a circle and relax, while sitting on the ground.

Sergeant White was brought to the field site to give the on consideration of others class, which surprised her. She started by telling them, "I didn't think I'd be talking to the same group again, about the same issue." She picked out Private Hilton at random and asked, "Who would you like to help you if in trouble in combat?" Before she could answer, she moved the question to Sharon and Private Whitt. No one answered. "Anyone? Do you think you'll care what color or creed a person is when you need help to survive? Believe me you won't. Now if what I say is true and I can see by the nods you agree, who still believes the race of a person matters?"

Travis uttered under his breath, "It has its place."

She challenged him by asking, "Did you say something, Travis? And if so, please stand and address the class."

He stood and addressed the class by saying, "Look, we all know racism exists. I'm just a good old country boy who was taught to accept it."

Malcolm said, "Elaborate, old enlightened one." with a sarcastic smirk.

Travis turned to him and replied in a violent tone, "I wasn't talking to you."

Malcolm replied with a stern tone, "So what? I was talking to you."

Sergeant White butted in and told them both, "At ease! This is exactly what I mean. You two acting like you'll tear each other's head off over a difference of opinion. We must remember that although we may not like what someone has to say, we must respect their right to say it." She then asked Travis, "Did you have more to add?"

He enthusiastically answered, "Yes. Now like I was saying, people like Malcolm, I mean minorities are always talking about racism and how they get the bad end of it, but it was the foresight of people like my father who made this country what is today. Where might I add, gave him the right to even dispute the fact."

Malcolm looked at him with an inner rage but refused to be lowered to his level. He simply said, "It would seem to me that in a country as great as America where a white male has every advantage and opportunity to be successful. If he finds himself poor, ignorant, and unsuccessful at the end of the day, there is no greater class of minority."

Travis turned to him with a grin and asked, "So what's your point?" ***Malcolm replies, "you just made it."*** Before anyone else could say anything, Jeff stood and asked Sergeant White for permission to speak. She granted him permission, and Travis smiled thinking Jeff will back him up.

Jeff started by saying, "I can see where Travis is coming from because I too grew up a good old country boy. I too was brainwashed with the same ignorance that pledges him now. I believe if something is forced upon you, you owe it to yourself to find out the truth. I won't lie, the road was rough for me and even still is today, but I'm learning more day by day and refuse to shut my mind to progress of any kind. I tell you from experience that racism has no place in this country or this army. If I can walk away with something, I will say to someone whom I regard as a good friend now that everything I heard about his race was wrong, dead wrong. I want to thank everyone here for the opportunity to train with, but especially you, Malcolm, you've helped me more than you know." He sat back down, and Sharon was almost in tears.

Malcolm walked over to Jeff. The two shook hands with an embrace and he told him, "Thanks likewise, man. I see you the same way."

Sergeant White told the class, "You all can learn a lot from their friendship because those were beautiful and very sincere words." The class was in awe and happy in a sense by Jeff's words. All except Travis, who now realized he had lost his best friend.

As the class was concluding, Sharon told Jeff, "I have something very important to tell you."

He eagerly asked, "What?"

"Wait until we are out of the field."

CHAPTER ELEVEN

Weekend Plans

They were released from class to go to lunch. They all sat talking about what will happen once they graduate since it's almost over. After eating, they headed back to the field site. Drill Sergeant Hansen called them to formation, "Field training is concluded. Once back at the company area, you will be released for a weekend pass. Don't party too much because first thing Monday morning, there will be a PT test for record. If you don't pass, you don't graduate. What needs to happen now is everyone needs to break down your tents and field gear and get ready for departure. Transportation will be here at 1800 hours so be ready. Fall out."

The soldiers returned to their rest area to finish packing. Everyone seemed to be in very high esteem, even Travis seemed happy, feeling like he belittled someone in the class. He and Jeff were within feet of each other when he asked, "I guess you hate me now, huh, since you are all righteous now?"

Jeff turned to him and said, "Look, I don't hate you or anyone for that matter. We just see things in different light. I know now that I can overcome anything, and that feels great. I believe there's even hope for you if you want it." He finished packing and added, "Good luck with your PT test and graduation." Then he walked off.

Malcolm, who finished packing earlier, used his extra time to write Michelle and tell her how hard it is for him being away from her for so long. He then heard the roll out call and headed for the departure area.

They all load up on the back of five-ton trucks and headed back to the company area. The ride took about forty-five minutes while they engaged in card playing and joking, excited to be going back where there is a shower and bed waiting for them. After the trucks came to a stop and they all off-load, there was a formation held. Drill Sergeant Hanson told them, "I am proud of this platoon for successfully completing your tasks. Tomorrow you will go on pass that will end on Sunday at 1700 hours. Now fall out and take a shower immediately." The soldiers all let out, "Hoo yah!" and rushed off to their barracks to put their gear away and shower.

As they started showering, twelve soldiers at a time, the rest waited impatiently, yelling for the first group to hurry up, and they were yelling back for them to wait. There was also a line formed at the phones where some soldiers were becoming unruly, but not violent. Malcolm and Jeff were in the second group to shower. They entered, and Jeff began to talk about Sharon, "I can't wait to spend time with Sharon. I just don't know what we'll do. I want to make the weekend special."

Malcolm offered to help. "Jeff, I bet you wonder what I'm doing sometimes when I'm up late at night."

"Yeah," Jeff said.

"I'm writing poetry. When we get back to the room, I'll show you some, maybe one will fit what you want to say to her."

"Man, you never cease to amaze me. Thanks." The two finished showering and headed back to their room.

Meanwhile Sharon was at her barracks with Private Hilton fumbling over the same insecurities as Jeff. She explained, "I am crazy about him, and everything must be perfect this weekend, or I will just die."

Hilton asked, "What do you mean? What do you want to happen?"

Sharon took a breath and said, "I want romance and mystery. I want him to wow me until I can't take it anymore then sweep me off my feet. I hope he's all I want him to be and more."

Hilton told her, "Slow down. He's just a guy. Don't set such high expectations."

"I know, I know," said Sharon, "but I think he is the one for me.

"Good luck," said Hilton.

Malcolm and Jeff were now in their room reflecting on their lives and how much they've grown. Jeff then took time to plan the perfect weekend, with the woman he's fallen in love with. Malcolm showed him a few poems to see which one he thought was the right fit. After he selected the perfect one, he went to the phone to make hotel reservations and ordered flowers to be delivered to the room. Malcolm was feeling a little lonely with all this romance in the air, so he went to the phone to call his love to see how her day is going. They talked about her class and her difficult midterms that are coming up.

As Michelle was talking, she noticed that Malcolm's spirits are down, and she asked, "What's wrong, baby?"

You see one of the things he loved about her was she could always tell when he was troubled, even when no one else did. He told her, "I will be glad when it's all over. Even though I've met some good friends, I really miss being with you."

"I miss you too, baby."

"I'll see you soon." Shortly after, it was almost lights out. He headed back to his room as Jeff was lying wide-awake, anxiously waiting what would happen tomorrow.

The sun rose that morning at 0630 hours. The birds were singing, and there was a big smile on Jeff's face, who was already in the shower. On a weekend pass, the soldiers were allowed to wear street clothing. Jeff chose a pair of casual slacks and a formfitting silk shirt for his date with Sharon. Sharon came down in a formfitting rayon knitted dress, which showed off her very shapely figure. As Jeff walked up to her, he was stunned again at her amazing beauty with the sounds of oohs and aahs from passing soldiers.

He asked, "Are you ready?"

She replied, "You're looking very nice."

He was thinking to himself, *You dummy*. To recover, he grabbed her by the hand, looked into her eyes for a second, and slowly told her, "You look absolutely beautiful today."

She smiled and said jokingly, "You say that to all the girls."

Jeff replied with a very serious look, "Oh no, believe me only you." Jeff turned and saw Malcolm walking by. "Hey, Malcolm!"

"Hey!" Malcolm said and gave Jeff a look as if to say calm down, you got it on lock, just relax.

He and Sharon headed to the taxi as if they were on their way to the prom. The first stop was a romantic restaurant that Jeff picked out. As they waited to be seated, there was a calm yet nervousness coming over them both. The waitress led them to their seats, telling them they made a cute couple. This helped to loosen them up and brought a smile to both their faces as they both replied thanks. They were sitting and looking at the menu for a selection and were continuously flirting with each other as they made their order. While waiting for their food, the conversation got serious. Sharon asked, "What are you looking for in a woman?"

He jokingly said, "Someone with all of your qualities." She repeated the question.

He saw she is serious and answered, "I'm looking for a woman that can make me smile when I'm at my lowest point, someone I can grow with and will love me with all her heart as I will do the same. Someone who won't give up on me ever even in my most stubborn state. Someone who will excite me sexually as well as mentally. I believe that is important so it doesn't burn out in a short time. Most importantly, loves me unconditionally."

Sharon smiled and said, "I guess you know what you want, huh? Good luck!" she jokingly replied.

Jeff, with a very serious look on his face, looked into her eyes and said, "I really hope that person is you."

Sharon was speechless, and her face began to blush. "Do you think you could love someone unconditionally in return?"

"If that person is you, without a doubt."

"Don't be so quick to say that because I feel the need to tell you something before we go any further.

"What is it?" he asked with a sound of concern in his voice.

She took a deep breath and, with the most serious look he had ever seen on her face, looked directly into his eyes and said, "I am half white and half black."

She paused as she look for any faint look of disgust or hate in his eyes. He said to her with a smile, "Is that all? I thought it was something serious."

A sigh of relief came across her face, and she asked, "Are you sure this will not be a problem for you?"

He grabbed her hand, looked into her eyes as if she was the only woman in the room, and said, "You know I've done a lot of growing here, and a lot of it has to do with you. So believe me when I say it doesn't matter what race you are because I fell in love with a beautiful woman the first time I saw her in the TMC. I don't plan on letting anything come between that. We clear?"

She replied, "Crystal."

The food arrived, and they sat gazing into each other's eyes, feeling closer than they had ever felt to one another. As they were eating, Jeff, with no warning, leaned over the table and laid a soft yet passionate kiss on a very willing Sharon, who gently grabbed the back of his head and laid a kiss of her own. After eating, they headed to a nearby nightclub where they danced the night away.

Jeff carefully told Sharon, "Don't worry I've taken care of the sleeping arrangements for the night.

"Oh really?" Sharon said, feeling turned on by his take-charge attitude.

"Yeah, and I hope that you will find everything to your liking."

"Okay then, I guess we can leave now."

Jeff agreed, and they left. They made it to the hotel door, and as Jeff reached to turn the key into the lock, he again leaned in and kissed her. As they passed through the doorway, Sharon's eyes opened twice the size as she saw a bed filled with rose petals and a huge box of chocolates. She ran to the bed and threw some of the petals into the air. As they fell to the floor, she told Jeff, "Everything is beautiful!" She then looked at him in a very seductive way. "Thank you." The two locked lips again; then she headed to the bathroom with her bags to change.

Jeff changed into his nightclothes as well. He put on soft music for background and now sat on the bed, reciting in his head the poem that Malcolm gave him, awaiting her return. The doorknob started to turn, and she walked out in a sexy long red nightgown with the back out and a slit up the side that revealed an even sexier red lace thong. Jeff was amazed again by her beauty, dropped the comb he had just picked up, and was instantly aroused by her. He tried to hide his nervousness with a macho persona. "You are breathtaking." Sharon blushed. He took her by the hand and walked her to the bed and sat her on the bed. Jeff then kneeled in front of her, looked deep into her eyes, and started to recite the poem:

When I first laid eyes on you, I thought it was a dream,
A beautiful face followed by style and grace as if something from a movie screen.
Though only in your medical care briefly you healed all my wounded parts,
But most of all you accelerated the beat of a lost yet yearning heart.
Over the past few weeks I know we've grown closer day by day
And I desperately look forward to knowing you better in each and every way.
The sound of your voice gives me goose bumps your touch paralyzes my soul,
Plus every waking moment thoughts of you strengthen and continues to grow.
When I thought I lost you my heart rate dropped below detection,
I'm so thankful for a mutual friend who pointed me back in the right direction.
The strength you have inspires me to be more of a man

And now that were back together I pray we never part again.
From the day I met you I've become a better man with no regrets,
So I wrote this poem to thank you for not looking away when our eyes first met.

As he was reading the poem, her eyes began to water, and she too became aroused. After he finished reading the poem, he told her he loves her. Sharon grabbed him and pulled him close to her, and the two engaged in very passionate kissing and lovemaking, which to them was almost cosmic. Easily the best lovemaking either of them had ever had. After a night of lovemaking and ecstasy, they fell fast asleep.

The next day, the sun rose to uncover a smile on both Jeff and Sharon's face. They lay, looking into each other's eyes, for what seemed like hours. Then the front desk rang to remind them that checkout was in an hour; they hurried to the shower together. As they were getting dressed, not many words passed between them.

Jeff broke the silence, "That was the best day and night of my life." Looking into Sharon's eyes, he said, "I love you," which surprised him as soon as the words left his mouth. She walked over and gave him a kiss, and they headed out to breakfast. After eating, they headed back to the company for the four o'clock formation. As they arrived at the barracks, the two of them parted ways. Sharon went to her room and Jeff to his.

As soon as she entered the room, she fell on the bed embracing her pillow where Private Hilton was awaiting details. "You are glowing. Was it a dream come true?"

Sharon let out a loud shriek and told her, "Yes, it was," and began to tell her the details. "I would have never thought of him as romantic."

"How so?"

"Girl, he brought flowers and chocolates on the bed. Then when I thought everything was as good as can be, he topped it by kneeling in front of me, reciting a poem about us. Wow, I just melted in his arms. He was nervous like a kid kissing for the first time. He was cute and gentle."

"Damn, sounds like you got your wish."

"And some."

"Yeah, I hope to find me someone soon, you know?'

"You will."

Jeff, on the other hand, walked in his room with a huge smile on his face. Malcolm said, "I take it everything went okay."

"That's an understatement."

"Did the poem work?"

"Like a dream, but I tweaked it a little."

"Then my work is done. You got her now. Good luck, my friend."

"Thanks, man. I couldn't have pulled it off without your help."

"Yes, you could have—just not as smooth." They both laughed. Jeff sat down with a puzzled look on his face. "What's wrong?"

"I told her I loved her."

"Did she say it back?"

"Not at first. She kissed me."

"How did you feel when you said it?"

"It just came out, but it felt right."

"Don't worry about it. Most problems occur when things are left unsaid. Now get changed we got formation in fifteen minutes."

CHAPTER TWELVE

The Final Test

They both prepared for formation and headed out bumping into Travis in the hall, who had cut off all his hair. He said, "What's up, bro?" Jeff just looked funny at Malcolm, who started a quiet laugh.

At that moment, the drills called out formation, and they all hurried outside. This formation was relaxing for most of the soldiers, knowing that the worst was over. In one week, they would graduate and become real American fighting soldiers. Drill Sergeant Hansen called them to attention then at ease, "It's been a long haul, but we made it together, and that's what counts. For a drill sergeant, there is no prouder moment than to see a recruit turn into a solider. Now back to reality. None of what you did up to this point will matter if you fail your PT test tomorrow. To put it plainly, you will not graduate. There will be one makeup on Wednesday, if you should fail. Fail the makeup and you will not graduate. So my advice to you is take this very seriously. On the command of fall out, I want you to go clean your room, take your personal time, and get some rest you'll need it. Fall out!"

Malcolm took the time to call his love to see how she's doing and wanted to ensure she will be at his graduation.

Jeff and Sharon sneaked away for a talk and a brief kiss before returning to their rooms. As Jeff headed back upstairs, he was approached by a skin-headed Travis who seemed to want to talk to him badly. Jeff asked, "What is wrong with you?"

"Nothing."

"Why did you cut all your hair off like that?"

"I'm just doing like them. I'm keeping it real."

"Whatever, guy. What do you want anyway?"

"Man, I'm worried about this PT test. I might not pass."

"What part are you worried about?"

"The push-ups and the run."

"Okay, let's go upstairs, and we'll work on your form for the push-ups. Plus if you can stay with me for the first mile of the run, you should pass. I'll help motivate you."

Travis replied, "Thanks, bro," and they headed upstairs.

Malcolm returned to his room and did a few push-ups and sit-ups of his own. He had developed a ritual in which he always did the minimum push-ups of forty-two and sit-ups of fifty-two and stretched the night before a PT test. This gave him added confidence going into the test.

Jeff gave Travis as much help as he possibly could before going to bed but was still doubtful of his chances. Before leaving, he told Travis, "Remember, just take it one event at a time. Don't think about anything but what you are doing at that time. You can't take that energy with you, leave it on the ground on each event. Give it your all, okay!"

"Yeah! Good luck and good night. I'm going to bed." The drill yelled "Light outs!" Most of the soldiers lay awake, thinking of the next day's events.

It seemed just as they closed their eyes for sleep it was time to awaken to a new day. Everyone awakened, eager to take on what will be their last challenge as a recruit. They all headed out to the PT test formation. Malcolm and Jeff, two of the highest scorers at all the events, were talking and laughing as they walked up not really concerned about the test at all. Travis, who was extremely nervous, was quiet for what seemed like the first time since he started AIT. As they stood waiting to start, the drills gave them their last block of instructions, and they formed lines to begin with push-ups.

Malcolm stepped up first, knowing he will have no problem with this event as he did one hundred easy on his last test. As he stepped up alone with several other soldiers in different lines, he noticed a very serious look on the face of his drill that was awaiting him. Malcolm got down into the push-up position and Drill Sergeant Hansen yelled, "Get set, go!" He and fellow soldiers began pushing up and down, up and down. Suddenly Malcolm continued to hear his drill count one, one, one, so he stopped and asked, "What's the problem?"

His reply was, "You're not going down low enough." Malcolm, feeling this treatment for being too cocky, was not about to let this stop him. So he started again bouncing his chest against the floor to prove a point and still finished with eighty push-ups.

After watching Malcolm slightly struggle, who easily did more push-ups than anyone in the company, the recruits quickly realized that this was for keeps, and a newfound fear set in. A number of soldiers went before Jeff, who has no problem finishing with seventy-five push-ups of his own. Travis was up next with his palms sweaty. The drills told them to get into the start position. The sound was yelled, "Ready, set, and go!" He began pushing almost unsteadily out of breath due to nervousness. Jeff was watching and encouraging him to push himself to the limit. Travis finished with forty-four; two more than the amount needed to qualify.

They all breezed through the next event, which were the sit-ups with little or no problems. And now came the run, which is the final event and all that stood between them and graduation. The soldiers headed to the start point, nervous yet anxious. While walking to the start point, a timid Travis came up to Jeff to remind him to run with him, "No problem. Just relax," Jeff said as he continued joking with other soldiers.

At the start point, Drill Sergeant Hansen went over the rules for the course, "This is a two-mile run, one mile up and one mile back. Words to remember, if you don't make it in time, you don't graduate, so leave it all on the course and push yourself." Before starting, they got a brief rest to stretch and loosen up in preparation. They moved in the start position, Travis clinging close to Jeff in hope for some serious moral support. Hoping to find a way to do what he had been unable to do for the last PT test, pass the run. The drills yelled out, "Get set!" They took their positions. "GO!" They all took off with a lighting burst of speed. Malcolm led the pack with a few other soldiers, who cruised the course with little difficulty if any at all; Jeff, who normally would be in that pack as well, stayed back to help push Travis. The pace was fast and fierce with an every man for himself mentality on the minds of most soldiers. As Malcolm finished the first mile and headed back, he began to look for Jeff as he got farther and farther toward the end. As Malcolm was approaching Jeff and Travis, he yelled, "If you don't pick it up, you won't even qualify!"

Jeff heard this and realized he hadn't even finished his first mile yet and yelled at Travis to speed up, but Travis was full of excuses.

Malcolm yelled again, "Come on, Jeff. You didn't come all this way to fail."

Jeff heard this and took off, leaving Travis behind who slowed even more. By now, most of the male soldiers have finished and some females as well, and most have passed Travis by now. Jeff came in slow as the drills yelled out, "One minute!" Malcolm, who was long finished by now, ran out to push Jeff in an all-out sprint to the finish line. He crossed as the drills yelled out, "Thirty seconds!" but was too tired to go back and help Travis who was far away from the finish point. As the time expired, Travis, along with three other soldiers, failed to finish on time. Travis went into an anger-type trance and instead of blaming the person responsible, which was himself, he choose to direct his anger at Malcolm for telling Jeff to leave him behind. He crossed the line and gave Malcolm a look that could cut steel.

Malcolm simply laughed, called him weak, and walked off. The soldiers all headed back to their respective platoons to hear their confirmed scores of all three events. Drill Sergeant Hansen called them to at ease and congratulated them on a job well-done and a great effort put forth. He also informed the soldiers who failed that there will be a makeup test on Wednesday, and that would be their absolute last chance to pass. They were released from formation to shower and change and was given the rest of the day as personal time. Sharon and Jeff agreed to meet up after their shower to visit the PX together.

Malcolm headed to the phone to let his mom and family know he had made it through.

Travis still feeling down in his self-pity, pledged to get revenge on Malcolm, whom he again blamed for something. As the majority of the soldiers sat around the common area, they began talking about where they would like to be stationed and shared thoughts on what it would be like.

Jeff went to Travis's room, trying to lift his spirits. "I'll run with you on the makeup test."

Travis just laughed in a very demonic way, saying, "That isn't necessary. This is not the life for me, and I know that now."

"What? What do you mean?"

"Listen, Jeff, you are of pure blood, so I can't hold anything against you, but you are proof that this is a corrupt way of life. You have turned your back on everything. You were brought up to believe and for what, to become friends with a nigger and a zebra chick?"

Jeff grabbed Travis by the throat and drew back his fist with a look of fire in his eyes. Then he stopped and said, "You know what, you're not even worth it. I feel sorry for you. Have a nice life. I don't want to ever see or hear from you again." He then walked to the shower to calm down.

On his way, he bumped into Malcolm. Noticing a disturbed look on Jeff's face, he asked, "What's up?"

Jeff replied, "Nothing," continuing on and bursting through the bathroom doors.

Malcolm walked by the room he came out of, seeing a very disturbed-looking Travis sitting on the bed with his head down. He simply shook his head and walked on.

CHAPTER THIRTEEN

A Coward Flees

With an air of happiness over the camp, everyone was eagerly awaiting their new orders, which will tell them where they will be stationed. They were all resting, lounging around the common area, playing pool and watching TV. By now, Jeff has calmed down and was chilling with Sharon, talking and kissing.

Malcolm called his love to let her know what's going on; she told him how proud she is of him and all he's done and how much she loves him. They were planning where they want to live, both hoping for him to be stationed on the East Coast, preferably Georgia, where she is in school. With forty-five minutes before lights out, they exchanged their good-byes and I love you's and got off the phone. Malcolm hung up and headed to dayroom. As he entered, he saw Travis off in a corner all to himself. He noticed that the TV was on a channel no one seemed to be watching but Travis, who was there first. Malcolm endured it for a moment then asked, "Is anyone really watching this because there's a game on."

He heard an overwhelming, "Change it" from the soldiers.

One voice came from the back of the room, saying, "Leave that TV alone, boy." Malcolm turned to look back, seeing who made the comment, and noticed it was Travis. Instead of getting upset, he simply replied as he turned the channel, "It's no wonder he doesn't want to see people running since he can't seem to do it." All the soldiers began to laugh.

Travis said, "You black fuckers are probably born with basketballs in your hands. It's a wonder your mother could even give birth to you."

Malcolm became upset by the mention of his mom. He simply told Travis, "Watch your mouth."

"Why, you don't want me saying something about your mommy, huh?" Malcolm turned and looked at him with a look that could cut steel as if to say one more word.

Travis, with hesitation in his voice and fear in his heart, saw Jeff walking by and uttered the worst words you can say to any man. "Fuck your mom!"

Before he could even finish the statement, Malcolm threw the chair he was sitting in at him. Travis ducked the chair, but as his head came back up, it was greeted with solid right cross, which dropped him back to the floor. Soldiers quickly grabbed Malcolm, who fought his way through them and continued to punch Travis. Jeff ran in and grabbed Malcolm and calmly said, "We are about to graduate, he's truly not worth it." Malcolm looked at Jeff, pushed him off, and walked out. The soldiers all headed to their rooms because it was almost lights out anyway.

As the lights go out, Malcolm and Jeff were having a brief conversation about what life is going to be like as a regular soldier. At the same time, Travis has packed his bags and slipped off post to a nearby bus station where he purchased a bus ticket and headed home.

The next day was fast upon them, and most soldiers were already awake in anticipation. Jeff couldn't help noticing as he passed Travis's room that his bed was made, but his boots, which he should've been wearing, was still under it, but thought nothing of it and continued to formation. That morning there were two formations, one for the graduating class and one for the retest. The idea was to have the entire class root them on so they will pass. As they did roll call, there was one soldier called out of rank. The squad leader identified him as Private Travis. The drill sergeant ordered the squad leader to go upstairs and get the soldier. As the soldiers waited, he returned with a report that not only was Private Travis gone, but his wall locker was empty and all his personal items had been removed. This didn't surprise Drill Sergeant Hansen. He then ordered the squad leader to fall back into formation. He then reported Private Travis AWOL to the MPs, and they continued with the day's scheduled events. The next order of business was to complete the PT test. Once administered, it was a complete success. All retry soldiers passed the test. They were then ordered to join their fellow soldiers in the proper formation. As the formation was dismissed, they all headed to chow. On the way, Jeff began to speculate about what happened to Travis. Jeff asked, "You think he really left or is just playing around somewhere?"

"No, I think he left. He did what all cowards do when the going gets tough—they run away and hide."

"Whatever he did, it was stupid."

"Man, he isn't really worth talking about." Jeff agreed, and they continued on to chow.

CHAPTER FOURTEEN

Graduation

It was now time for graduation. Neither Jeff nor Malcolm's parents showed up, but Sharon's mom did make the trip. She was so proud of her little girl and equally as happy that she had taken interest in a white young man. Although she couldn't keep her eyes off Malcolm, admiring his chocolate skin tone and muscular body. She would continuously find reason to touch him as they all walked to a nearby restaurant for dinner. As they sat eating, word had come that they were going on Code Red for Kuwait. They immediately rushed back to the company areas. Once they were back, their orders were to pack their bags and get into battle dress uniform. As they rushed anxiously and nervously toward their rooms, they began to speculate.

Jeff asked, "Do you think it's real?"

"Yeah," replied Malcolm.

"If it's real, are you ready?"

"I won't be any more ready tomorrow."

Jeff looking puzzled, shaking his head then asked, "What?"

Malcolm seeing how worked up he was becoming, said, "Yeah, but, man, just relax. Let's see what's going on first."

Sharon told her mom good-bye and got ready.

They all returned to formation, scared yet proudly awaiting instructions. Drill Sergeant Hansen gave them a very inspiring speech and let them know up front that this was not a drill. "Because of your training and skill level, some of you will be going directly to Kuwait while others will report as scheduled to your regular duty station. Before I read the names, let me say it was my honor to have trained you, and I would gladly battle alongside anyone of you here today." A lump grew in their throats as he read off the names, "Turner, Wilson, Whitt, Chavez, Norton, Jeff, Malcolm, and Hilton. If your name was not called, you can stand down; your existing orders still stands—you will report to your assigned duty station. If your name was called, you need to double-check your gear, call home, and take care of any personal things you need to because you have been selected to report to Kuwait. There will be a briefing in two hours. God bless you and good luck. At ease."

After formation, the soldiers sort of stood around in disbelief of what just happened. Most were very relieved their name was not called and happy to be stationed in the United States. The soldiers' names that were called were proud and scared, not knowing what to expect. They rushed off to call their loved ones and informed them of the news.

Malcolm called his mom, and she broke down crying while he delivered the news, saying this was her worst fear come true. He told her, "Don't worry. I'm coming back home. The way I see it, surviving the streets of Detroit was a war in itself, this can't be much harder." He ended the conversation by telling her, "There's no way I'm not coming back."

Jeff, on the other hand, took it very badly; tears filled his eyes as he called his mom. She tried her best to comfort him. His dad asked for the phone. He simply said, "Son, pull yourself together. Men in this family stand strong."

Meanwhile, Sharon was running around frantic, looking for Jeff and Malcolm. She saw Jeff sitting off into a corner alone with his head down as he tried to come to grips with what's going on. Sharon called his name, but he didn't answer at first, then he slowly looked up at her. She rushed over to him. Seeing his extreme discomfort, she just wrapped her arms around him and began crying herself. Jeff was so moved by her actions; he touched her very firmly, gently to lift her head by her chin. He then looked directly into her eyes. "I don't want to leave anything unsaid." She waited patiently to hear what he had to say. "I love you, Sharon, and I really wanted you to know that before I leave."

Sharon gave him a kiss. "I love you too, now more then ever. Stop sounding like it's the end of the world. You will come back to me, and we will be together."

"I hope so, Sharon . . ."

Sharon quickly replied, "I know so because I love you that much." As she said that, Malcolm walked up. She jumped up and gave him a big hug.

She can tell how he's hurting, but the tough guy that he is, he'll never show it. "How you doing?"

"Just ready to get it over with."

Sharon can tell he's a little scared but respected his strength in the face of adversity and knew Jeff will need him when times get rough in Kuwait. She took them both by the hand. "I want you two to stick together. Promise me you'll stick together no matter what." She then looked at Malcolm. "Please bring my baby back to me in one piece."

He saw the pain in her eyes. "Don't worry I won't let anything happen to him."

"Promise me."

"I promise." He then looked at Jeff. "Come on, you'll be fine and so will I. Now let's go to formation and find out what's our next move." Jeff stood and passionately kissed Sharon, and the two headed outside.

Attention is called to the small group of soldiers selected to deploy to Kuwait soil. They stood proudly awaiting orders. Drill Sergeant Hansen called them to at-ease position before giving the instructions. "It's okay to be afraid. It is a normal emotion. The important thing is that fear is a reminder to stay alert, never quit. Remember your training and you'll be fine. That being said, you will be confined to the company area for the rest of the night and will deploy at 0415 hours. You will link up with Alpha Company already on the ground in Kuwait. There is two hours before lights out so use it wisely. God bless you and good luck. Attention! Fall out."

As they headed back to their barracks, Sharon grabbed Jeff by the hand and accompanied him to the TV room where they began to embrace and kiss. Malcolm was also in the TV room sitting and talking with Private Hilton, who was growing fond of him. Sometime while watching TV, all the deploying soldiers came together and began to talk with the exception of a few nondeploying soldiers. They formed a sort of a pack with a promise to always watch each other's back, no matter what and shook on it. They all exchanged personal information—home addresses and phone numbers and next of kin; this would ensure they will always be able to find one another. Sharon exchanged with Jeff, Malcolm, and Hilton, promising to write them all. After this was complete, they all headed back to their rooms for lights out. Malcolm and Jeff lay awake most of the night waiting and talking, reflecting on how far they both have come, kidding each other and even joking about. They started telling each other what they thought of the other the first time they met. Jeff said, "I thought you were some ex-gangbanger, who thought the world owed him something."

Malcolm was saying, "Yeah, and I thought you were some confused little mommy's boy, who wouldn't last the first week. I never thought we'd be here."

"Never thought my best friend would be . . . ," he pauses, "from Detroit."

They both started to laugh. Their eyes slowly shut shortly thereafter.

They were awakened by their new NCOs (noncommissioned officers), ordering them to grab their gear quickly and head to the trucks. As they left, a strange feeling came over Sharon as if she knows Jeff's gone; she simply shed a tear and turned over in bed. They made it to the airport and, in minutes, took off. The flight took a long thirteen hours where mostly the soldiers sat in silence watching movies and receiving briefings on the status of the Gulf War and the role America is playing in it. They were informed of the importance of what they are doing—protecting freedom and rights of others. They finally touched down and quickly saw that this was real and not a joke. The environment was intense and very combat-ready. It was extremely hot and had the appearance of a giant desert.

CHAPTER FIFTEEN

The War

The trip from the airport to the new unit was fast and direct, with a low detection rate. They were herded into the back of a few five-ton truck and were driven two hours to their destination. Once there, they teamed up with other soldiers that had been there for months and were getting edgy. To put it shortly, there was no welcome speech. Jeff, Malcolm, and Hilton stuck close together as they were being assigned to their units. They all managed to stay in the same unit, but Hilton was placed in another squad. The other soldiers were split up into other platoons. Once they received their sleeping arrangements, Malcolm and Jeff were sleeping side by side. They also received a briefing and were assigned duties. During the briefing, they realized how real the threat was being given the signal for gas and having to get into mock 3 (full chemical protection gear) in a hundred-degree weather. They were also told of the importance of staying in their designated areas and not to pick up foreign objects off the ground or any surface. The reason was these may be bombs or some type of chemical agent. The briefing was closed with a statement that had to be drilled into their heads since they joined the military: stay alert and stay alive. Then they were dismissed.

They were to wait for further orders from their commanding officers. For the first three or four weeks, they were sent on recon mission, scooting out the terrain and reporting enemy activities. By day they humped, and by night, they took cover as they watched the night skylight up from the many missiles fired at Iraq. They would be out days at a time, scouting and running into a sandstorm, forcing them to take cover. The storms were so violent at times it would rip the flesh from their body if exposed too long.

After being there for about three months, it was obvious that America would win the war.

One day, while out on a routine scout mission, Malcolm and Jeff, in a squad of ten soldiers, with Sergeant Thomas as the squad leader, ran into trouble. About three miles into it, they saw in a far distance enemy activity. They began to approach the area using extreme caution. As they closed to within a quarter mile of the location, they noticed a celebration around a burned U.S. Hum-V. It seemed they had ambushed some American soldiers and were excited by it. This sent a sense of rage and pride through the squad all at the same time. Without the use of words, Sergeant Thomas ordered them to move in on their position. They began final approach, locked and loaded with live ammo. As they raised their weapons to fire, Malcolm noticed one of the enemy soldiers coming from the right with his weapon aimed at Jeff. Malcolm broke silence, yelling for Jeff to get down as he took aim and shoot the soldier. The gun battle ensued; Jeff, who barely escaped death, was now pinned behind the burned hum-v. Each time Jeff attempted to move, they shoot very close to him, letting him know that if he moves an inch, they got him; but they weren't trying to kill him at this point, they are just using him for bait. Malcolm has found cover behind a nearby sand dune where he was in direct communication with Jeff, who was very afraid.

Malcolm told Jeff, "Calm down and don't move. I will get you out."

"Malcolm, please don't leave me, man."

"Never. Now stop talking crazy."

Sergeant Thomas called for the squad, "Back off and find cover." They all complied with the exception of Malcolm, in fear that if he gave up his position, they could easily move in on Jeff with a straight shot, and he was not about to let that happen. Sergeant Thomas called out to Malcolm again, "Back off and find cover!"

"What about Jeff?"

"Don't worry, we'll figure something out."

This wasn't an acceptable answer for Malcolm, so he held his position and told the sergeant, "If I move, they'll kill him for sure."

He was again ordered to move back, which he not only ignored, but also advanced closer to Jeff's location barely escaping the blaze of gunfire. This angered Sergeant Thomas but left him with no choice but to lie down cover fire for them both.

Malcolm told Jeff, "Get ready to move, I'm coming to get you. We can shoot our way out. I know where they are positioned."

"I think my leg is broken."

"Can you stand on it?"

"I think so," replied Jeff.

"Well, get up, and let's get ready to move. You can hurt later. On the count of three, start firing on the nearby sand dune. That's where most of the enemy soldiers had taken cover behind. One . . . two . . . three." Jeff began to fire as Malcolm dashed to his side, taking a bullet in the arm in the process. He helped Jeff to his feet, and they began to move in a straight line using the hum-v for cover as long as possible. Then when they had a clear moment, they dashed into a foxhole that was next to them. While this was under way, it gave Sergeant Thomas the distraction he needed, sending three remainder of the squad to flank the enemies' position, leaving some of them dead and wounded while others surrendered and were brought back as POWs.

Once back at the camp, they received medical attention and were released shortly after. Malcolm had a superficial wound to his left shoulder, and Jeff had an ankle sprain. Sergeant Thomas greeted them upon release from medical care. "How are you feeling?"

They both replied, "We will be okay."

He then ordered Jeff back to the tent while pulling Malcolm to the side to talk. "You disobeyed a direct order. Do you know what that means?"

"Yes, but I meant no disrespect to you . . ."

"Save it and just listen. We all have rules to follow. It's what keeps things in order. When we fail to follow them, people die. Although what you did should be commended, you jeopardized the lives of my entire squad. One day, you'll be put in charge of the lives of soldiers, then you'll understand my position."

"Will I be kicked out?"

"Now that would be an injustice to the US Army. I believe you are a good soldier. As far as I'm concerned, this will go no further than this conversation we are having here. Now go to the tents. You guys should be receiving orders by morning on your new duty station."

"You mean we are going home?"

"Yeah, back to the States, it's almost over here. Units have already started to deploy home."

"Okay!" Malcolm headed to the tents excited, holding his arm.

"Hold it, soldier!" Sergeant Thomas stopped him for a second saying, "You've earned my respect today, I was very proud of your bravery." The two exchanged a mutual head nod, and Malcolm walked off.

When he made it back to the tent, he and Jeff began to talk about what happened.

"Man, you really stuck your neck out for me."

"It was nothing. You would have done the same for me," Malcolm replied, downplaying the situation.

"No, man, I'm not joking, this is serious. I mean I hope I would have done the same, but no one really knows what they might do."

"That's real."

"I owe you my life. If ever you should need me for anything today or years down the road, just let me know. I mean it. You saved my life, I won't ever forget that."

"Man, I was just trying to keep a promise I made to a friend." The two shared an emotional moment and embraced in a brief hug. Just as they sat back down, Sergeant Thomas came in to tell them to report to formation in fifteen minutes.

"There will be a briefing on the status of the war, and some of you will be receiving orders on the spot, others will receive them in the morning, but we are all going home."

The soldiers yelled with excitement, "Hoo yah!"

CHAPTER SIXTEEN

Orders to Return

The next morning came, and they received their orders; both were to be stationed at Fort Hood, Texas. They shared a joy in going to the same place, and it's also where Hilton is going and Sharon is stationed. They began to pack their field gear and read their letters—each one has a letter from Sharon. Malcolm has one from his love Michelle, so he went off to himself to read it. Hilton walked over to him, jokingly, asking "What's the secret?" He smiled and walked off. The next day, they were put on a plane and were sent to Fort Hood. They were processed and assigned to a new unit again. The two of them were placed in the same unit and company area. After Malcolm and Jeff settled in, Sharon stopped by and picked them up to show them the area base. That night, they all went out, and Jeff and Sharon can't keep their hands off each other. They were at the sports bar having a few drinks when Hilton made a pass at Malcolm. "Would you like to leave with me tonight?"

He smiled and said, "Under any other situation, I would love to."

Her face turned sour as she asked, "But . . ."

"But I have a very beautiful lady whom I love very much. She's been on my team for far too long, and I could never forsake that trust."

Hilton was hurt but admired him even more for what he said, saying a silent prayer to find a man like him one day. "You'll always have a friend."

"The feeling is mutual." The two hugged and continued to party a little longer then headed their separate ways. Malcolm headed home to call Michelle.

Jeff and Sharon, on the other hand, had left the club and were catching up in their hotel room. They were engaging in passionate lovemaking for hours, then lay together, confessing their love for each other. Sharon shed a tear, telling Jeff how much she worried about him. He shared with her the story of how Malcolm saved his life. They continued talking and embracing until they fell asleep.

Malcolm was also sharing his story of Kuwait with his love over the phone, who was planning to come visit him soon.

They were now settling in their units and beginning their new jobs, also meeting new soldiers they will be working with. Malcolm was excited about Michelle's visit in a couple of months.

Sharon and Jeff were engulfed in the love they shared for each other and were even talking about the possibilities of a life together forever. After being there for a few weeks, Malcolm purchased a new car, and he and Jeff were looking at it over and began to talk.

Jeff asked, "When do I get to meet this Michelle I've heard so much about?"

Malcolm smiled and said, "She'll be here this weekend."

"Oh yeah? That's why you been acting so nervous lately."

"What? I'm as cool as a fan."

"Okay."

"On a serious note, I'm going to ask her to marry me."

"Man, are you sure?"

"I've never been surer of anything in my life."

"I've never seen you like this before, so she must be someone special. You know if you need me in any way, just let me know."

"What are you talking about? You're my best man."

Jeff stood speechless, very honored that Malcolm would want him to be his best man. "It's funny because I feel Sharon may be the one."

"Oh yeah?"

"Yeah, she's got my heart."

"That's good. I think you two will make a good couple, and you know I'm here for you as well."

"You know if it goes that way, I can't think of anyone I would want on my side that day but you."

"I'll be right there."

"So, Mr. In Love, what you got planned for her visit?"

"Well, I don't want to plan too much, just keep it as natural as possible. The most important thing for us is our time together, that's all. I'm going to take a two-day pass and go to San Antonio for a weekend."

"That sounds like a good idea. Maybe Sharon and I can go."

"Hey that's cool, let's do it."

They made plans and headed back to post. As they were working and living in a peaceful environment, they noticed a large degree of racial separation within the post. It seemed that most of the officers were white and most enlisted soldiers were minority. Most of them, like Malcolm and Jeff, came from poor backgrounds, trying to make a better future for themselves. They don't put too much focus on it and easily accept this way of life. Remembering that they are there for a reason as well, and they will not be sidetracked. During the next couple of weeks, Malcolm and Jeff were hanging out together more and more at the clubs, working out together at the gym and even work. Sometimes Sharon and Hilton hang out with them as well along with a few new soldiers they meet. Now the time has come for Michelle to visit, and Malcolm was excited. He and Jeff went over their plans one last time with Sharon present, who was so happy for Malcolm.

She told him, "I can't wait to meet Michelle. I can't wait to meet the woman who caught your heart."

Malcolm just smiled and said, "She'll be here tomorrow."

CHAPTER SEVENTEEN

The Visit

Malcolm went to the airport to pick up Michelle on Friday morning, standing at the terminal, waiting to catch a glimpse of her exiting the plane. Michelle stepped off the plane wearing a very nice formfitting sundress, showing off her beautiful shape. She spotted Malcolm, dropped her bags and ran over to him, giving him a big hug and kiss. They exchanged I love you's and how much they missed each other, then headed to the car where Malcolm had flowers and chocolates ready for her. He took her on post to meet Jeff and Sharon, filling her in on them along the way.

Once there, he introduced them, and they each gave Michelle a big hug, saying to her, "There are no strangers here, just family."

"Thank you. I heard so much about both of you, I guess I should also thank you for looking out for my baby and keeping him out of trouble." She smiled at Malcolm.

Jeff said smiling, "It was no problem. It was more him saving my neck."

Malcolm jumped in and said, "Okay let's get this show on the road." They loaded up the car and headed to San Antonio.

After arriving, they quickly checked into their hotel where Malcolm and Michelle stayed for the entire night. They stayed in their little love nest and spent the whole night talking, making love, and ordering room service. Michelle's eyes filled with tears. "I was so afraid something might happen to you while you were away. I truly could never imagine my life without you." As tears rolled down her face, she said, "I love you so much."

Malcolm wiped her tears, telling her, "Your love kept me strong, and there is no way I am not coming back to kiss your beautiful lips again." They made more love until they fell fast asleep.

The next day, they woke up and took a romantic walk along the Alamo, talking and hugging tight. They stopped at a nice place on the way to have brunch. After eating, they ran into Jeff and Sharon, who joined them for a boat ride along the Alamo. This gave Sharon and Michelle the chance to talk, and they all became closer as friends.

Malcolm told Jeff, "I'm going to pop the question tonight at dinner."

"Good luck, my friend. She is a keeper and a very beautiful woman."

"Thanks." They headed to dinner.

Malcolm picked a beautiful spot with a view of the city and a live band playing inside the restaurant. He thought this was the perfect place to ask her. As they were sitting, waiting for the main course to arrive, the band all of a sudden stopped playing. This got the attention of the entire restaurant. The bandleader grabbed the mic and said, "We have a special request from a very special guy here tonight. We ask that you please be patient as I turn over the floor to him." The band started to play a soft, smooth jazzy beat; and as they started to play, everyone was looking around to see what's going on.

Malcolm stood and kneeled in front of Michelle as the bandleader handed him the mic.

When I first laid eyes on you, it seemed my heart had just been caught,
For your explosive and amazing beauty through my eyes had no faults.
Your hair full and black with the appearance of butter silk,
Your eyes were hypnotic, and I was drawn to your lips.
Your legs, a chiseled sculpture, perfect in design,
Your body is that of a goddess with an equally matching mind.
You say the things I love to hear and hear what I love to say,
That is why the love we share has grown so strong and strengthens with every passing day.
You send chills down my body as if I was a circled pole,
You rush blood from my heart stimulating parts unknown.
The world you are to me, my picture of life and all that matters,
And I would hold you in my arms forever, if it means our dreams would never shatter.
Every time I lie down next to you, I want to fill your love from within,
And if your love was somehow taken then I could never love again.
The reason I'm pouring my heart out to you is because I cannot live without you in my life,
And on my knees I nervously ask, will you be my wife?

Michelle started to cry, looking into his eyes and was very excited, repeating, "Yes! Yes! Yes! I love you!" The entire building stood and started to cheer for them. As Malcolm read the poem, there was a hush about the room. Other men watched, admiring Malcolm's courage. The women sit, some wishing to be in Michelle's place, others hoping they were asked in a way as romantic as that. After she accepted, they started to kiss and danced the night away. Many people came by to say congratulations, how beautiful the poem was, and that they made a great couple.

Meanwhile, Sharon and Jeff sat at the table, admiring and feeling closer than ever, even wishing it was them getting married. After finishing dinner, they headed back to the hotel for a night of passion, completely absorbed in each other.

The next day before heading back to post, Malcolm and Michelle called their parents to tell them the good news. They got back to post and said their good-byes as Michelle had to get back to school. Malcolm planned to take a leave in a few weeks so they can go home together. Jeff was also planning to take a leave with Sharon so that she can meet his parents.

They continued on with their everyday life as soldiers. One night, shortly after Sharon and Jeff were having a conversation, Jeff asked, "What was life like for you while growing up?

She looked at him and said, "Honestly, pretty well I must say. Except the fact that there is a whole other side of my heritage that I know nothing about."

"How do you feel about it?"

Sharon was surprised and happy that Jeff had taken such a genuine interest in her past life. "Well, it makes me feel incomplete. All my life I've been accepted as one way. I'm not complaining. My mom was doing what she thought was best at the time, but I would like to meet my father one day and know if I might have brothers or sisters."

"You will then and I'll help, if you'd like."

"That is so sweet. Thank you," Sharon said and kissed his forehead. "How about you? How was your upbringing in Kentucky?"

"Painful."

"How so?"

"Well, my father is a racist. He used to get drunk and occasionally hit my mother, and when I was old enough to stand up to him, he started hitting me too. I saw him do things that frightened me beyond words." Sharon could see the hurt in his eyes as he was talking. "You know I love my dad, and I remember when we were so close, but I wish he didn't hate so much. I've learned that no matter who you hate, it seems to always come back to hurt the ones you love. When we go on leave, it is important to me that you meet my family."

"It's important to me too." They embraced in a big hug and headed to bed for the night.

The weeks passed quickly up until their leave date. During that time, Jeff asked Sharon to marry him, and she accepted, so it's a celebration of sorts as well. They all took their leave time together. Malcolm agreed to drop them off on the way to pick up Michelle.

The night before they left, Jeff and Malcolm got out for drinks. Malcolm asked, "So when did you pop the question?"

"It was nothing as creative as your proposal was. We were sitting at the table eating, and I just asked and she said yes."

"That's great! Congratulations! I'm sure you'll be very happy together. I was thinking . . ."

"What?" asked Jeff.

"Since I'll be driving through redneck-ville, you ever hear anything about Travis?"

"A couple guys I know say he's working at the local factory now, and he even went to my house and met my pop."

"Oh really?" asked Malcolm.

"Yeah, I am sure they'll get along fine. Travis is the kind of son I think he wanted."

"So my question to you is, you sure you want me driving you home?"

"Man, yeah, my parents already know about you, I told my mom and dad. The way I see it is we are family now—they can accept it or not. It doesn't really matter to me."

"Yeah, but is it safe?"

Jeff saw Malcolm was really bothered by this. "I promise you this, nothing will happen to you that doesn't happen to me first."

"Okay I'll take you at your word." The next day, they packed up and headed out on their trip.

CHAPTER EIGHTEEN

The Long Trip Home

They hit the road happy and joking around, reminiscing about basic training and AIT. Making fun of their favorite drill sergeant, Sharon joked about how stubborn the two of them were and so set on proving who was tougher. She then said, "All joking aside, I'm so glad we got tight, I couldn't imagine getting through it without you two by my side. Especially you, baby," kissing Jeff on the cheek.

Malcolm jokingly said, "Hey, no mushy business 'til we get there."

Jeff turned to him and jokingly said, "Aw, you feeling left out?" and played at giving him a kiss. Malcolm pushed him away.

They made a few rest stops as they drew closer. Malcolm noticed Nazi symbols on the walls of the restrooms accompanied by some racial slurs. He said nothing of it. As they continued on, word has traveled that Jeff was on his way home. Word had even pierced the ear of Travis who was in the next town over. Travis, not knowing Malcolm would be with Jeff, planned to greet him, in hopes of renewing a friendship.

They finally arrived, and Malcolm was feeling uneasy as Jeff introduced him to his family. Jeff's father was reluctant to speak, his mom seeing how nervous Malcolm looked, she quickly grabbed him by the hand and led him into the house for something to eat. As family members and friends filed in and out of the house, they couldn't help but notice how beautiful Sharon was. The men were staring, and the women turned their nose up as they slapped their husbands and/or boyfriends. Travis saw Malcolm with Jeff and decided not to greet him, returning home instead, furious. He returned home very angry as he remembered all the negative things in his life to blame black men for. He then planned his revenge. He took a rifle out and loaded it up and said to himself with a dreadful gloss in his eyes, "I will make him pay."

After dinner, Jeff, his mom, and Sharon convinced Malcolm to stay, which was against his better judgment of planning to be clear of this town before nightfall. Jeff began to share his stories of Kuwait with his family, proclaiming Malcolm as a hero.

Malcolm attempted to downplay his role by saying, "We were all both brave and afraid."

Jeff, having a little too much to drink, stood up and said, "No! No! I will not let you downplay this; the truth is, if it weren't for that man . . ."—pointing to Malcolm—"I would not have made it back home."

This got the attention of his father who asked, "How so?"

"Well," Jeff explains, "I was pinned down behind a hum-v with enemy fire all around. My squad leader ordered everyone to pull back, leaving me there alone. Malcolm disobeyed a direct order, ran to my position, pulled me out, and laid cover fire as we ran to safety, even taking a bullet in the process."

His father simply looked at Malcolm and said, "Oh yeah?" and walked out of the room with cane in hand.

Jeff told Malcolm, "Don't mind him."

Meanwhile, Sharon was engulfed in a conversation with Jeff's mom Mary at the dinner table. It's getting late, and Mary explained the sleeping arrangements. Sharon was shown to her bed and quickly fell to sleep. Jeff and Malcolm stayed up on the front porch, drinking and talking. Mary, before going to bed, came to the porch with the boys and told Jeff, "Your friend came by, but I guess he left before you got here."

"Who?"

"Travis. He said he went to basic with you."

Jeff replied, "Yeah, but he's no friend of mine. How many times has he been by here?"

"I'm not sure, once or twice. He and your dad talked in the yard. Well, I'm going to bed, just thought you should know. Malcolm, make yourself at home."

"Thank you for your hospitality."

Jeff and Malcolm headed to bed shortly thereafter. While they lay asleep, peaceful in their beds, Sharon and Jeff wrapped tightly in each other's arms, Malcolm lay half asleep and half awake, still feeling not quite comfortable there.

Meanwhile in the next town over, Travis was awake, planning to kill Malcolm, loading his rifle. His plan was to shoot Malcolm in the morning, seeing this as the perfect revenge. He left just before sunup and picked a tree about thirty meters in front of Jeff's front door. There, he waited for his shot. This same tree was what Jeff had used as a child to hunt small game because it proved a great cover.

The next day came and Malcolm was eager to get on his way, after talking to Michelle. Mary told him, "I know you don't think you're getting out of here without breakfast?"

"No, I wouldn't think of it," Malcolm said with a grin on his face.

They all sat at the table, eating and talking, while Jeff was telling more stories about his childhood. While eating, a neighbor came by to tell them, he saw someone snooping on their property early that morning. Jeff's father Bill said, "Oh yeah?" and grabbed his rifle and headed to check things out. By now breakfast was over, and they all walked out to the porch to wish Malcolm on his way, pausing briefly to convey good-byes. Travis peeked out, viewing this as the perfect time to get him; but as he shifted his position, a bird flew out from the tree and caught the attention of Jeff. Jeff looked, seeing something wrong and took a closer look, discovering it was Travis with a gun. "Everyone, get down!" he yelled. Malcolm turned, and Jeff saw that Malcolm was his target. He dashed in front of Malcolm, catching a bullet in the back. Bill, seeing where the shot was coming from, returned fire, causing Travis to drop his rifle and fall from the tree. He tried to run off but was hit in the leg by the second bullet fired by Bill. Jeff lay bleeding on the ground as Sharon and Mary were in shock, yelling for help. Malcolm also in shock, managed to call 911.

Bill walked up to the shooter and kicked him over on his back only to discover it was Travis, the kid claiming to be his son's friend. He asked him "*why*?" not knowing his son was shot.

Travis said, "I was trying to kill that nigger because he is evil."

Bill looked at him with the gun to his head and suddenly saw Jeff's face on Travis's body and, in a fright, jumped back. Thinking to himself, *This in not what I wanted my son to become*. He took the rifle from Travis's head and said, "No more hate." and walked back to his house.

The police came and picked up Travis just as Bill discovered that it was not Malcolm who was shot but his son Jeff. Bill dropped his rifle and fell to his knees and begged for forgiveness from God, hoping his son's life will be spared. Malcolm saw this and offered Jeff's father a ride to the hospital, which he accepted. Mary and Sharon rode in the ambulance, praying the entire way. They arrived and waited as the doctor performed an emergency surgery on

Jeff. He successfully removed the bullet from his back as his family waited for him to regain consciousness. The doctor came in and said, "Jeff should pull through. He lost a lot of blood, and he needs rest."

They went in and visited him, praying and hoping he wakes up soon. Each one was saying a few words in Jeff's ear and moved on, leaving time for his mom and dad to be alone with him.

Mary stood silent, and Bill apologized to both her and Jeff. "God, please bring my son back to us in good health. I was wrong, so very wrong in many of my attempts to teach my son what being a man is. I truly thought what I was doing was right and would toughen him up as my father did to me. I know now that if I had succeeded, I would have created a monster full of anger and hatred as I have been for far too many years."

"Son, I am sorry, I really am. Here I am thinking I was the teacher, and I learned the most important lesson from you."

As the last words left's Bills mouth, Jeff's eyes slowly opened and he replied, "It's okay, Dad, I forgive you."

Tears streamed down Mary's face, both for her son and her husband, as she was moved so very deeply by their words.

"I love you, son."

"I love you too, Dad." They embraced in a family hug.

Sharon and Malcolm sat, waiting and talking in disbelief with what happened. Sharon was crying and telling Malcolm, "I hate Travis. I want to kill him."

"Yeah, we share that feeling."

Mary came out, "Jeff is asking for you." Malcolm went in, and they left them alone to talk. Bill was tear filled as he walked out.

The room was silent as a very humbled Malcolm walked over to Jeff. "I can't believe—"

Jeff interrupted him, "Man, I love you like a brother. There was no way I would've let that coward shoot you like that."

Malcolm said, "So you jumped in front of a moving bullet? You are out of your mind." They both smiled. "Man, I will never forget what you did for me on this day."

"I just returned the favor. It is funny how life works out."

"How so?"

"Well, I joined the army to get away and meet people who thought differently than I have been taught. I never thought in a million years I would've met my brother."

"I feel the same." Then the two embraced in a hug.

Just then, Sharon walked in and said, "Where's my hug? I love you so much." And Sharon started to kiss all over Jeff's face. Malcolm sat in a nearby chair, joking and laughing with them both. Sharon continued to cry and kiss Jeff until other relatives came into the room.

Malcolm went back to the lobby and saw Jeff's father Bill sitting alone. Malcolm said nothing, just sat to himself and picked up a magazine to read.

CHAPTER NINETEEN

Will You Wed Here?

Bill came and sat next to Malcolm. "I'm sorry."

"For what?"

"I judged you before I even knew what character of man you were, and I was wrong, dead wrong."

Malcolm tried to quickly dismiss it, saying, "Don't worry about it, no big thing."

Bill insisted, "It is a big thing. I've judged far too many people in my life, and I pledge never to do it again. It is this same hatred that almost caused my son his life, in the hands of another that thought as I did." Malcolm just listened as he can see Bill has something on his mind. "If my son thinks enough of you to jump in front of a bullet, then I was the fool for not seeing it myself. You saved my son's life once, and for that, I am forever indebted to you. I do ask a favor of you, a small token to make this right."

"How so?"

"My son tells me you are also getting married."

"Yeah."

"I would be honored if you would do it here."

"Are you serious?"

"I am very serious, and I will help fly your family here, if you need it. Just please don't refuse me this honor."

Malcolm paused for a moment and said, "Let me talk to my family about it."

"Okay," replied Bill. He then stood teary-eyed and extended his hand to Malcolm for the first time. Malcolm stood pulsing slightly, looked into Bill's eyes and shook his hand. Then Bill hugged Malcolm with his other arm, thanked him and walked humbly to his son's room.

Malcolm told Sharon, who was excited by the idea. He then went to call his love and told her about the proposal; she was leery at first but said she trusted his judgment completely. He then phoned his mom, who was very worried after hearing all that's happen down there.

"Baby, what do you think? Because I've known a lot of people like him in my days, and I don't know one person that has changed."

"Mom, he seems very remorseful. I think in a way he wants this to be some kind of redemption for his past or something.

"Do you believe he's sincere?"

"Yeah, I do."

"Is it what you want to do?"

"I wouldn't mind it."

"Okay it's your day, do what your heart tells you. Is it safe for us to come there?

"I believe it will be. I have to go, but I'll check around and ask some more questions and be sure."

Before getting off, she said, "Baby, whatever you do, be careful."

"I always am, Mom."

He went back into the room with Jeff, who has already heard the news and asked Malcolm, "Are you going to do it?"

"I don't know yet."

Jeff said, "Look, man, I know it's a big deal. Hell, our lives before the army was like night and day, all because we had a misunderstanding of each other's culture and background. Just think, if we can change, then maybe there's hope for the world."

Malcolm smiled and said, "I didn't know you were so poetic."

"What you think, you're the only one? It runs in the family," said Jeff with a smile of his own.

"Okay. Let's set a date."

"No problem. Next month."

"You sure?" asked Malcolm.

"I'm sure."

"Well, let's get the ball rolling then. I didn't get a chance to thank you for saving my life."

"Hey, man, don't mention it, just repaying a favor."

Malcolm headed out of the room. "Malcolm," Jeff called, but he just looked at him.

Malcolm stood looking back, then said, "Me too." and walked out.

In light of all that happened, the military had no problem granting them an extension on their leave. During the next two weeks, Malcolm drove home, picking up Michelle and his mom. Other family members flew. Sharon's mom and other family members also flew in. By now Jeff had healed up nicely, and they all started doing pretrial wedding runs. With just one day before the date of June 1, they all went to the church and prayed as one family.

Bill stood. "I am happy to see each and everyone of you here today. As we all stand united here in the house of God, I have a few things I'd like to say, if you'll all bear with me please. I have done things in my life that now I feel ashamed and embarrassed to admit. I have been a racist, a poor husband, and a bad example as a father. I say before God and all of you here today, I am sincerely sorry. I followed some bad examples that led me down a very hateful road. I understand now that it is love that makes you strong, and I love you all." Mary moved to his side as he was tear filled. "They say a father should be wiser than his son, but it was my son who has taught me about love, and I am eternally grateful. I also wanted to thank Malcolm for allowing me to host this very special day in the life of his family. From this day forth, your family is my family, and I love them equally. I'm not going to be long-winded, I'll end by saying God is truly great, and may he bless this union of combining all the families here as one. Amen."

The families returned his amen, and they all walked out to where there was food and refreshments waiting.

The next day arrived, and it was beautiful. The birds singing, the sun bright and shining, and the grass was green and as soft as a bed of carpet. They had the chairs assembled in the front yard where the family was sitting and waiting for the brides and grooms to enter. Malcolm and Jeff took their place at the altar and awaited their beautiful brides. "Here Comes the Bride" began to play, and the two beautiful brides began down the aisle hands interlocked. Many people were stunned at their beauty, as if they were seeing them for the first time. They made their way to the altar, stopping beside their grooms as the music was called to a stop.

The pastor began with the vows as the four of them stood, clutching hands. He asked, "Do you take Malcolm and Jeff to be your wedded husbands?"

"I do," replied both.

"Do you take Sharon and Michelle to be your wedded wives?"

They also replied, "I do."

"Then by the power vested in me, I now pronounce you man and wife. You may kiss your bride." They both lifted the veils and delivered the most passionate kiss they had ever exchanged in their lives. Before leaving on their separate honeymoons, they took time to greet and meet each other's families while sharing brief stories of how they became friends.

Malcolm and Jeff sneaked away for a moment to talk before leaving.

Malcolm said, "I now believe anything is possible, and I thank you for that, Jeff."

Jeff said, "What, you thank me? I wouldn't be here if it wasn't for you. You're like a brother to me."

"What do you mean? We are brothers."

"I know, that's what I just said." They both laughed it off. The two embraced for a moment, tears filled their eyes as they said their brief good-byes. At that moment, their new wives arrived to take a picture, both saying this will be a picture they will share for a lifetime.

THE END

MISUNDERSTANDING

M—MAINTAINING MENTAL DISCIPLINE
I—ILLUSTRATE INTELLIGENTS
S—SURRENDER SUPERFICIAL OUTLOOKS

We as a people are missing each other by way of connection/communication, without the (MIS) we have (Understanding).

Through understanding one another we can learn from one another and have unity and peace. I impress upon you these simple and humble words. The world has only one people," you and me". **(*A child's prayer*)** Let us forgive the past misunderstandings and petty differences of this world's history and truly become one nation under god . . .

UNDERSTANDING

U—Uses intelligence, temperament and patience when making decision affecting others.
N—Needs no acknowledgement for doing the right thing
D—Demonstrates the characteristics he/she expects from others
E—Earns the respects of others by first giving respects to others
R—Rigorously fights until the results are achieved
S—Stands on the side of righteousness even when it is not a popular choice
T—Teaches others knowing we are stronger together
A—Aggressively pursues answers even when the questions are yet to be asked
N—Navigates change from the front
D—Demonstrates courage under pressure
I—instinctively aids and helps when needed
N—Never waver from what is right
G—Great people

Positive Quote; If All Men Were My Brother And All Women My Sister Then who Would Be Left To Be My Enemy . . .

BY

MR EUGENE O CHARLEY